— The Cartoons of —

EVANSVILLE'S KARL KAE KNECHT

HALF A CENTURY *of* ARTISTIC ACTIVISM

JAMES LACHLAN MACLEOD

THE History PRESS

Published by The History Press
Charleston, SC
www.historypress.net

First published 2017

Manufactured in the United States

ISBN 9781625858382

Library of Congress Control Number: 2016953494

For Jessica, Eilidh, Calum and Gavin, the loves of my life.

Contents

ACKNOWLEDGEMENTS

This book was only possible with the help of those local archivists who protect our precious historical legacy. I would like to acknowledge Tom Lonnberg, Pat Sides, Kathy Bartelt, Shane White, Steven Mussett and Jennifer Greene, all of whom have graciously helped at various stages of this project. This book is built on the pioneering work of Dr Phil Ensley, which was what first drew my attention to Karl Kae Knecht.

The Karl Kae Knecht Collection at the University of Evansville Archives was an incredible and essential source for this work. I also acknowledge the Evansville Vanderburgh Public Library; the Evansville Museum of Arts, History and Science; the Willard Library; and the University of Southern Indiana, whose physical and digitized collections of local newspapers, artifacts, photographs and cartoons from this period made this research practical. I am extremely grateful to them all for permission to reproduce the images that appear in this book.

I would also like to thank my colleagues in the History Department of the University of Evansville and Dr. Ray Lutgring, dean of arts and sciences, for their advice, support and encouragement. An arts, research and teaching grant from the University of Evansville supported some of my research. Drew Robards was a wonderful research assistant, working on the World War II cartoons, and Ed Mack has been a thoughtful and helpful editor at The History Press.

Most of all, I want to thank my own family, who now know more about Karl Kae Knecht than they ever wanted to. To the four of you, with my warmest love, this book is dedicated.

It goes without saying that any errors in this book are my own responsibility.

INTRODUCTION

The great American cartoonist Syd Hoff once said, "Not everybody can love a political cartoonist. If you want to be loved by everybody, don't become a political cartoonist."[1] This certainly seems to be advice that applies in almost every case, but one clear exception to this rule is the *Evansville Courier*'s editorial cartoonist Karl Kae Knecht. "An intensely human man who never let praise go to his head,"[2] Knecht seems to have been someone who was loved by everybody; indeed, the editorial comment in the *Sunday Courier and Press* the day he died began with the words, "I never heard anybody say a word against him."[3] On "Karl Kae Knecht Day" in Evansville, July 21, 1954, nearly five hundred people at the Vendome Hotel came to their feet and roared their approval when the *Evansville Press* columnist Bish Thompson declared, "Through his newspaper work, a daily visitor in our homes for 48 years, Karl Kae Knecht, friend to all men, friend to all animals; a man who never did a mean thing, or said a mean word, in his life...without a doubt, [he is] Evansville's most beloved citizen."[4]

What makes this truly remarkable is that Karl Kae Knecht was engaged for his entire professional life in a career that is almost synonymous with meanness and nastiness—a profession that has been called, among other things, "the art of ill will" and "the ungentlemanly art."[5] "It's my job, as a satirical cartoonist," said Martin Rowson, "to give offence."[6] On another occasion, Rowson said, "The idea of giving offence is integral to the medium."[7] Victor Navasky perhaps expressed it best:

> *Under certain circumstances cartoons and caricatures have historically had and continue to have a unique emotional power and capacity to enrage, upset and discombobulate otherwise rational people and groups and drive them to disproportionate-to-the-occasion, sometimes violent, emotionally charged behavior. I'm talking about everything from overheated and irrational letters to the editor and subscription cancellations to censorship, prosecution, incarceration, and...violence and murder.*[8]

Knecht's output of editorial cartoons was prodigious—he had created at least eighteen thousand by the time he retired—and furthermore, he drew the vast majority of these cartoons for one newspaper in one city. It seems almost incredible that this could be done without making lifelong enemies in a city that was at times famous for its dirty and ruthless politics, and yet Karl Kae Knecht managed to do it.

He drew his first daily Evansville cartoon for the *Evansville Courier* on September 29, 1906, and his last regular one on June 1, 1960, and during the fifty-four years in between, his cartoons became an integral part of public life in the city. One of his obituaries stated that his "Triple-K Initialed cartoons were synonymous with The *Courier* for more than 50 years."[9] He was widely known as "the dean of American cartoonists" and was, for example, introduced that way at the 1960 meeting of the Association of American Editorial Cartoonists.[10] Knecht's cartoons appeared on the front page of the newspaper nearly every day until 1952, thereafter running inside, usually on the editorial page. He was nominated for a Pulitzer Prize in cartooning in 1944–45, and according to the historian Phil Ensley, "his fifty-four year career with [the *Courier*] was the longest tenure of any cartoonist drawing for a single newspaper in the history of American cartooning."[11] The collections of the presidential libraries of Theodore Roosevelt,

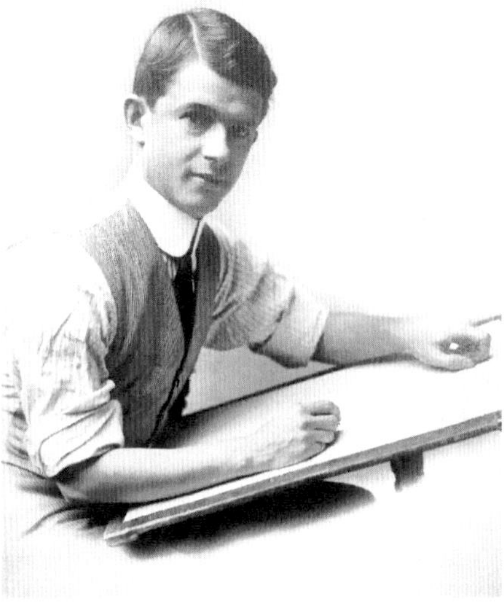

Karl Kae Knecht at his desk, 1906. *University of Evansville Archives (UE).*

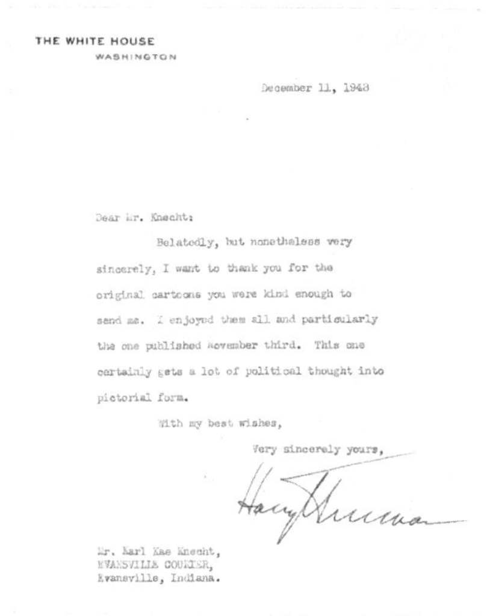

THE WHITE HOUSE
WASHINGTON

December 11, 1948

Dear Mr. Knecht:

Belatedly, but nonetheless very sincerely, I want to thank you for the original cartoons you were kind enough to send me. I enjoyed them all and particularly the one published November third. This one certainly gets a lot of political thought into pictorial form.

With my best wishes,

Very sincerely yours,

Harry Truman

Mr. Karl Kae Knecht,
EVANSVILLE COURIER,
Evansville, Indiana.

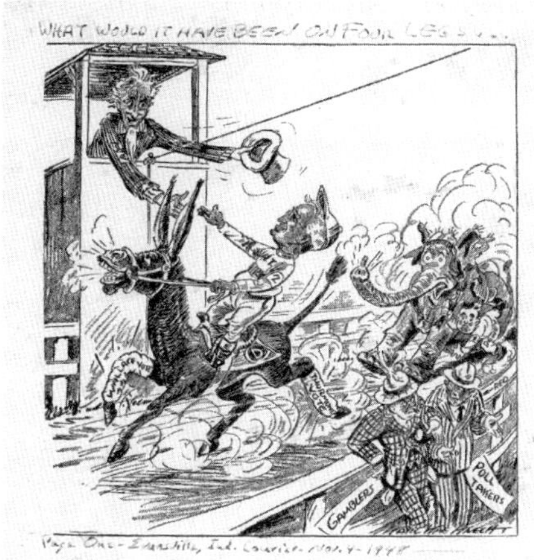

A letter from Truman in response to one of Knecht's cartoons, December 1948. *UE/ Evansville Vanderburgh Public Library (EVPL).*

Herbert Hoover, Franklin D. Roosevelt, Harry S. Truman and Dwight Eisenhower all include Knecht cartoons; the Truman Library has thirty-six of his cartoons in its collection. A recent edited collection of Truman cartoons from distinguished cartoonists based all over the country includes no fewer than nine by Knecht.[12] As can be seen, Truman wrote to Knecht to thank him for the gift of one particular cartoon in 1948. His scrapbooks contain letters of appreciation from the British queen, senior White House officials, governors, congressmen and judges, as well as notes signed by H.M. Warner of Warner Brothers, Nelson D. Rockefeller and Jimmy Hoffa. He might well be the only person who ever received complimentary letters from both Rockefeller and Hoffa. David Low, then of the *Manchester Guardian* and quite possibly the greatest cartoonist of the twentieth century, said of him in 1954, "Long may he continue to enjoy the regard and appreciation earned by his kindly personality and long career as [a] political cartoonist."[13]

What made Karl Kae Knecht such a remarkable man was that he was a rare polymath who excelled in many different areas. He was not just a cartoonist, then, but also a pioneering photographer, a fluent writer, a circus enthusiast, a zoo proponent, a champion of air travel, an effective organizer and a successful campaigner. He had a "phenomenal" memory—his friend and colleague *Courier* columnist Joe Aaron said of him in 1960, "He comes as close to being a walking encyclopedia as any person I have ever met. He is a complete reference book on Evansville, dating back more than half a century."[14] He even ran for the Indiana legislature in 1928 as a Democrat; it is perhaps fortunate for Evansville that this was the year of the infamous Hoover landslide, as Democratic presidential candidate Al Smith, a Roman Catholic who opposed Prohibition, led the party ticket to ignominious defeat nationwide.[15] It might be argued that his failing to achieve elected office was the best thing that could have happened for Evansville, as it allowed Knecht to focus on all the other things he was to do.

As much as anything, Karl Kae Knecht was an extremely potent activist for the interests of the city of Evansville. His good friend, the great Evansville civic leader Benjamin Bosse—mayor from 1912 until 1922—famously said, "When everybody boosts, everybody wins," and Knecht was a lifelong booster for his adopted city.[16] When Knecht boosted, everybody in Evansville won. Phil Ensley said in a 1995 interview, "Although he was a remarkable cartoonist, I would say that Karl Kae Knecht's greatest contribution was not to the world of cartooning, but to the city of Evansville. He supported almost every major civic organization and institution in Evansville—partially through his cartoon work—but also in his life. He was a 'booster' in the real sense of the word."[17] On his death, the *Sunday Courier and Press* observed:

> *During his 53 years as a cartoonist for* The Evansville Courier, *Mr. Knecht toiled incessantly for the benefit of Evansville and the Tri-State area. His accomplishments were so manifold casual acquaintances found it difficult* [to believe that] *they all stemmed from this slight, gentle man who somehow found time from his regular chores at the newspaper to found an international organization of circus fans, help start and develop Mesker Zoo, serve on various city and civic boards, travel extensively and become involved in scores of projects for the betterment of man.*[18]

It is quite possible that his only flaw in the eyes of those who knew him was sending illegible editorial copy to the *Courier* composing room—the printers' committee complained in 1952 about trying to read "some of the copy Knecht sent out which was first typed and then changed in many places in longhand."[19]

Karl Kae Knecht, who had a lifelong love of elephants, was so well known in his adopted city that in 1936 a piece of mail was received at the post office that simply had a drawing of an elephant on the front, along with the names of the city and the state: "With naught but an elephant, it was delivered to Karl Kae Knecht, the *Courier* cartoonist."[20] He was active in many different aspects of public life, but it is as a cartoonist that he is best remembered. And it is his cartoons that are the focus of this book. His professional cartooning career spanned a remarkable time in history, beginning in the Progressive era and not ending until the birth of the modern age in 1960, with Prohibition, the Great Depression, the two world wars, the Cold War and much else in between. In 1995, it was said of his work:

> *Karl Kae Knecht's drawings, graphic and full of detail, moved* Evansville Courier *readers with pictures of human frailty and need. He scolded bad drivers and spotlighted corruption. He poked fun at current events, boosted the community when things were bad, and alarmed the public to issues that affected their health. Knecht pressed many an issue in his 54 years with the newspaper. During wartimes he caricatured national leaders and commented on world politics. During campaigns and elections, he depicted local and national figures as he saw them, making observations on what they stood for.*[21]

The world that he entered as a cartoonist in 1906 was almost unrecognizable by the time he put away his pens, brushes and drawing table in 1960, and his cartoons are an enduring and important contemporary record of a changing world.

It might indeed be more accurate to say "worlds" rather than "world" because in many ways, Karl Kae Knecht was observing and commenting on three concentric worlds: Evansville, the United States and the wider global community. Sometimes his Evansville material paid no attention to the other two worlds—it could be intensely inward looking and local. As he wisecracked in 1955, "The average reader often loses interest in the United Nations or the cold war, but he's always interested when people start wearing shorts on downtown streets, etc."[22] Some of his cartoons dealt with American issues but had no international scope, while at other times, he took as his topic a foreign issue that seemed not to involve the United States at all. There were also moments when he spoke as a citizen of the world and did so eloquently and memorably—such as his cartoon from 1911 commenting on the sheer scale of modern oceangoing ships, in which a *Titanic*-style liner towers over the ghost of Columbus's *Santa Maria*. Another striking example is the January 31, 1948 drawing that marked the assassination of Indian independence leader Mahatma Gandhi: a plain white cloth with one bloodstain ascends to the heavens from India on beams of light. Of course his cartoons frequently straddled more than

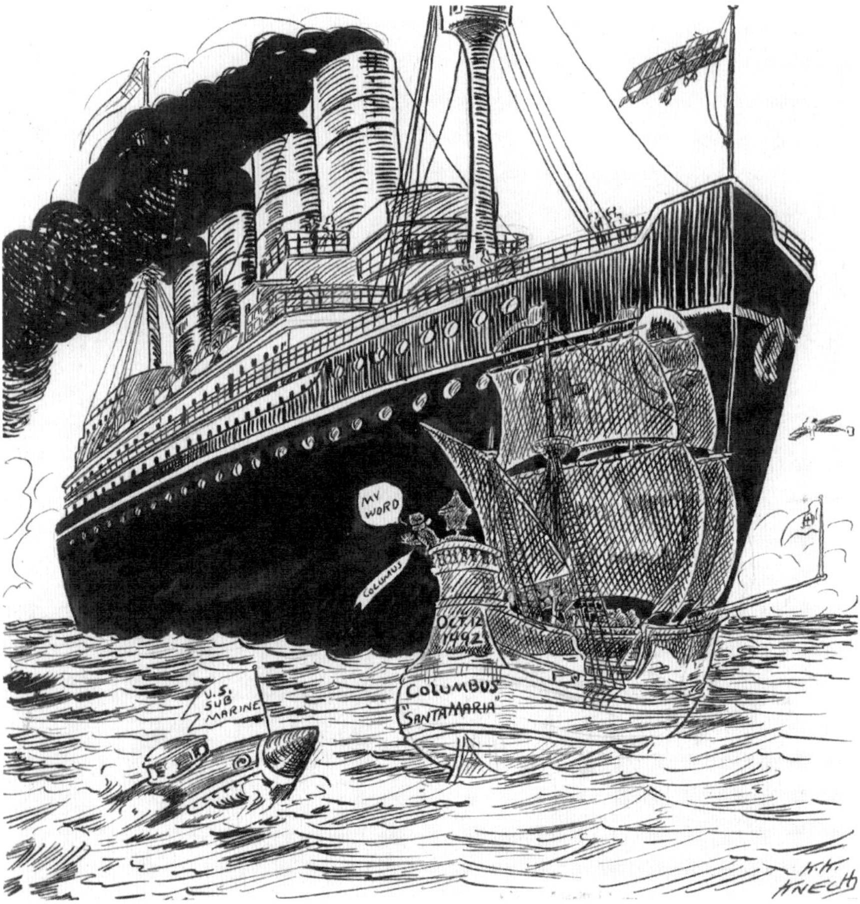

A vast modern ship contrasted with old ships, 1911. *UE/EVPL.*

one of these worlds, as many of his local cartoons were also a reflection of wider state or national or even international issues.

And then there were these moments when he managed to make the three worlds merge almost seamlessly. This is most unmistakably seen during the period that might well be Knecht's golden age—World War II—when he clearly believed that the smallest action taking place in Evansville was helping with the American war effort and, by extension, affecting the shape of the world that was to emerge from the war. Knecht's editorial cartoons during the war reflected a belief that the stakes were extremely high, and indeed, over the duration of the war his cartoons focused on the conflict almost every single day. They promoted activism in the sense that they frequently pointed out what readers could do and strongly urged them to

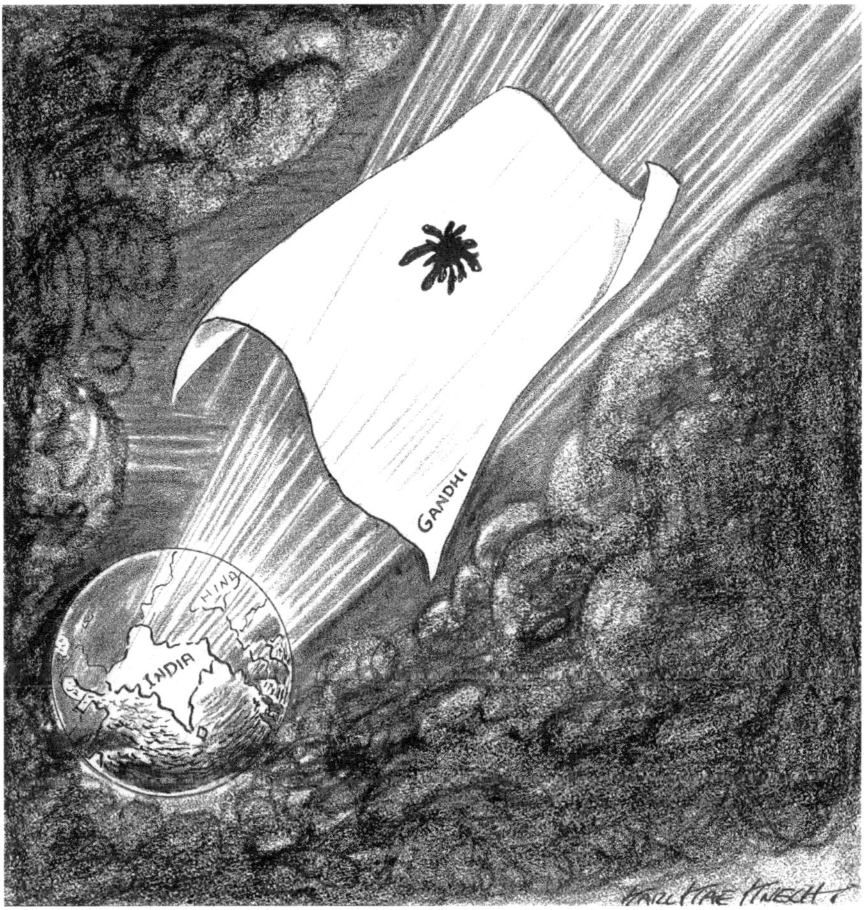

A bloodstained cloth marking the assassination of Gandhi, January 31, 1948. *UE/EVPL.*

do it. Crushing cans, collecting scrap metal, driving in a way that conserved tires, buying war bonds and even being quiet to allow night-shift workers to sleep were all things that he encouraged his fellow citizens to do to help ensure that the Evansville war effort, and therefore the American war effort, were successful and that the triple threats of Italian fascism, Japanese militarism and German Nazism would be defeated.

There was never any ambiguity about his view of these three enemies, either; the very first cartoon that he drew of all three after Pearl Harbor appeared on December 12, 1941, and depicted them as three of the most nefarious villains in literary history, under the caption "'Double, Double Toil And Trouble: Fire Burn, And Cauldron Bubble.'—Three Witches in

Shakespeare's Macbeth." It was a powerful and memorable image that underlined the seriousness of the situation; while many of his later cartoons would mock and belittle the three dictators mercilessly, this one emphasized the ominous power that they represented. Far from being objects of fun or derision, the three enemy leaders were sinister and terrifying; Hirohito and Mussolini in particular were the stuff of nightmares. This war, Knecht seemed to be saying to his readers, was going to be a battle against the forces of darkness. And there was no guarantee offered in this cartoon that the battle would be won.

As has been said, however, Knecht frequently lampooned the three dictators, presenting them as comic and unthreatening objects of ridicule,

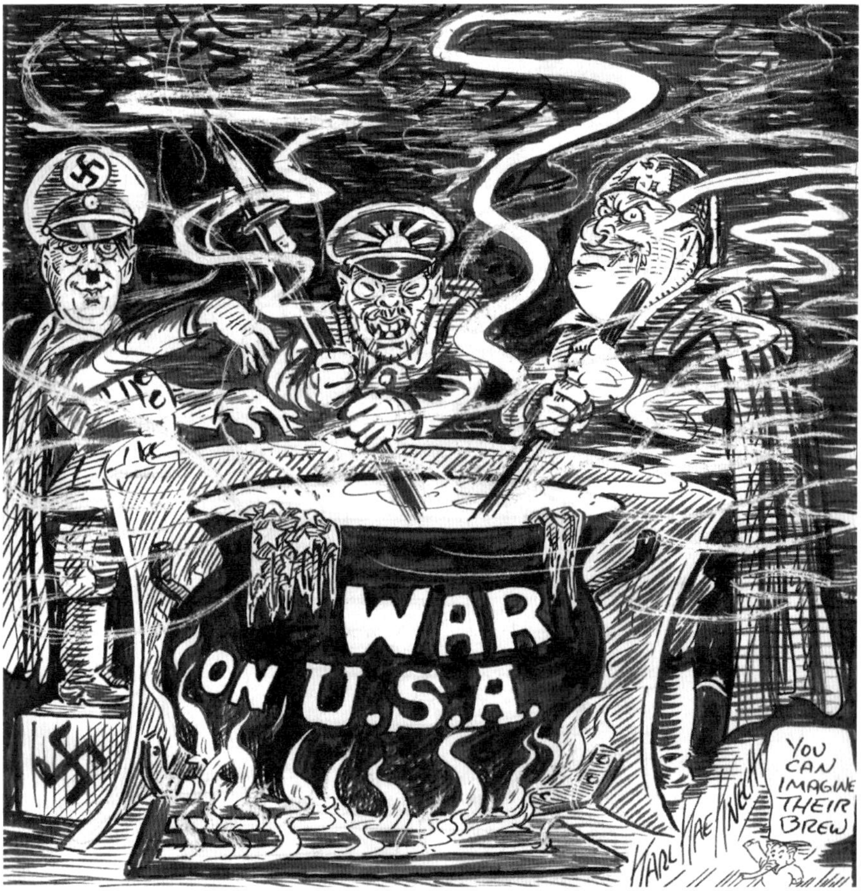

"'Double, Double Toil And Trouble: Fire Burn, And Cauldron Bubble.'—Three Witches in Shakespeare's Macbeth," December 12, 1941. *UE/EVPL.*

and this ability to project different tones at different times was certainly one of Knecht's greatest talents. Over the course of thousands of drawings and over seven decades, his cartoons were at times light and gentle and at others dark and harsh. He could be an impishly enthusiastic booster for the city and the country, but he could also be a fierce and relentless critic. He wrestled with the great serious issues of his time—war, the Great Depression, needless accidents, disease, Prohibition and political corruption—but he also drew numerous cartoons that celebrated civic pride, advertised local events and commented on whimsical little tidbits of trivia. And even on the most serious days, his trademark little elephant, named Kay, adorned a corner with an often funny comment or posture; she appeared almost every day from October 1928 onward.

A wonderful example of this is his first cartoon after Pearl Harbor, published on December 9, 1941, and captioned "Now then—All together." It is a powerful and prophetic image showing Uncle Sam, President Roosevelt and Knecht's Evansville everyman, Mr. Public—who for this occasion is labeled "Every American"—working in a blacksmith shop. Sleeves are rolled up, and their faces are stern as they labor in front of the fiery forge of war. Uncle Sam holds steady a piece of sheet metal that is labeled "Blue, White and Red" while FDR and "Every American" strike the metal with hammers. It should be noted how rugged the individuals look and that Uncle Sam and FDR appear to be much larger in height than "Every American." The cartoon is an excellent encapsulation of how the American war effort would indeed unfold—the country, the public and the federal government would roll their sleeves up and get on with the extremely difficult job of winning the war. This was particularly true in Evansville, where politicians, businesses, organized labor and regular people worked together extremely effectively to get a complex and challenging job done.[23] And down in the bottom right corner is Kay the elephant. She, too, is rolling her sleeves up and getting ready to help. It is a moment of gentle humor in a cartoon of considerable gravitas, easing the tension but also adding emphasis to the central point of the cartoon. It is classic example of Karl Kae Knecht's art.

It can be seen then, that understanding the work of Karl Kae Knecht involves the minute examination of his cartoons all the way down to scrutinizing what Kay the elephant is up to in the corner. To fully appreciate his work, however, it is essential to step much farther back and locate him in a wider context. In order to do so, this book will briefly discuss the history of editorial cartooning and will examine the work of some of the giants in the field. It will then consider Knecht's cartoons in a roughly chronological

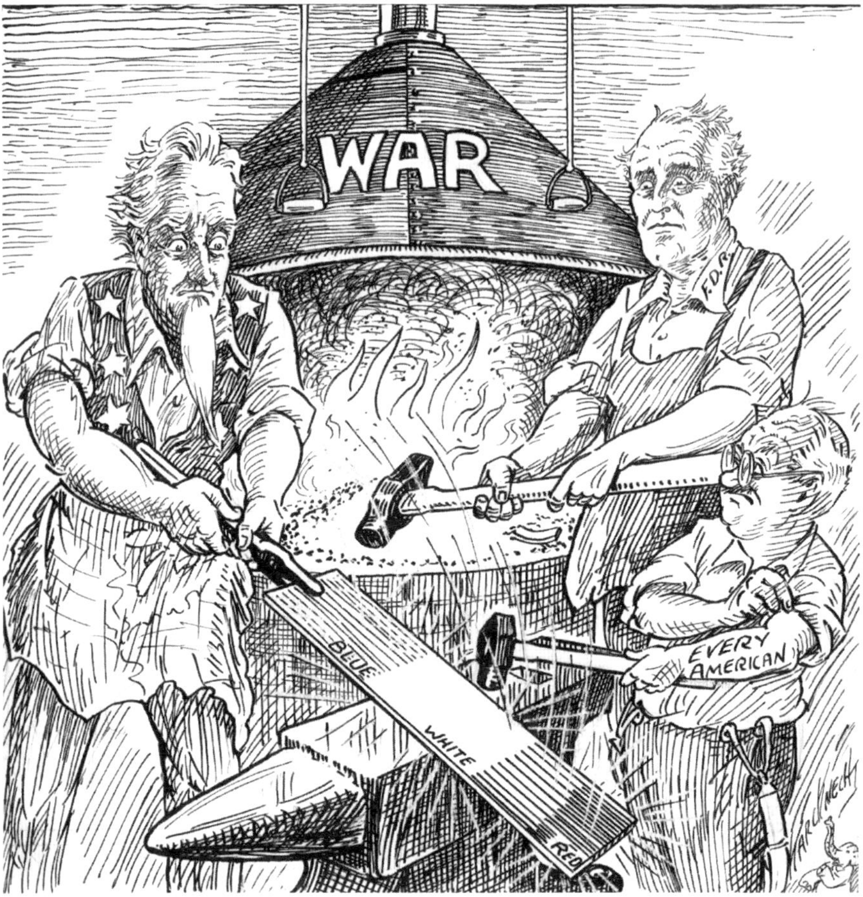

"Now then—All together," December 9, 1941. *UE/EVPL.*

manner, dividing his career into three stages: the first section will examine his work from the Art Institute of Chicago through his start with the *Evansville Courier* in 1906 until the late 1930s; the third section will study his art from 1946 until his last daily cartoon in 1960; and in between will be an analysis of his cartoon output during his golden age of 1939–45. As will be argued, this relatively short period was the most important of Karl Kae Knecht's professional life and, as such, deserves a more concentrated study than the other, longer periods. There will also be a discussion of Knecht's use of racist stereotypes in some of his cartoons and the context for that. Before any of this is considered, however, it is important to provide an account of his life and career, and it is with a brief biography that this book will start.

Chapter 1

The Life of Karl Kae Knecht

The son of Harry and Briget Knecht, Karl Kae Knecht was born on December 4, 1883, in Iroquois, South Dakota, a fact of which he was proud and to which he referred several times in his published art. His uncle Charles ran the general store, and his father—a quite accomplished artist—worked there; it is said that Karl was "the first white boy born after the town was started." The Dakotas were territories at the time and did not become states until six years after his birth.[24] He grew up and was educated in Freeport, Illinois, his father's hometown. Graduating high school in 1902, he moved to Chicago, where he worked for the Illinois Central Railroad. He then saved up his money to enroll in a course of study at the highly prestigious Art Institute of Chicago; he was to study there, with interruptions, between 1903 and 1906, and he published his first-ever political cartoon in the *Freeport Standard* on April 1, 1905.[25] On completion of the course, Knecht went to work on the night shift with the Wabash Railroad in Danville, Illinois. According to Ruth Ann Gregory, "During the days he slept little; [he] spent most of his time drawing up batches of cartoons which he mailed to newspaper editors all over the Middle West. One batch went to Victor Rosewater, editor of the *Omaha* [Nebraska] *Bee*, who recalled that Percy P. Carroll, Sunday editor of *The Courier*, was looking for a cartoonist. That's how Mr. K. and *The Courier* got together."[26] The editor told him that he liked his work and invited him to Evansville in September 1906.

Arriving at the rail depot at Eighth and Main Streets, he rode in a horse-drawn omnibus to the St. George Hotel with "nary an auto in sight." He spent

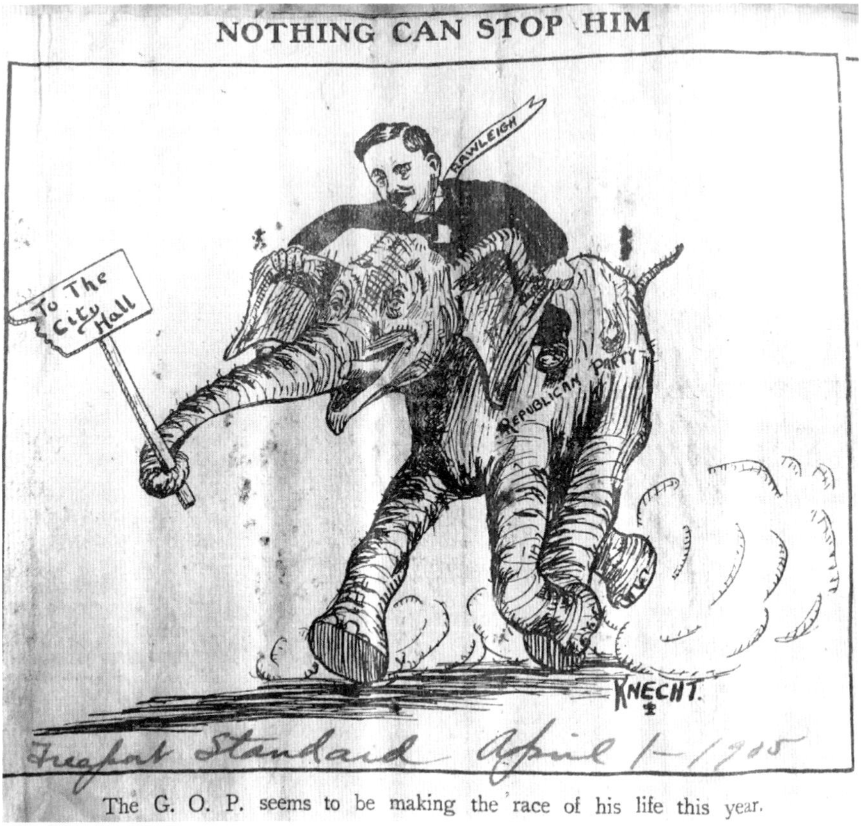

Knecht's first published cartoon, April 1, 1905. *UE.*

his first evening in Evansville at the theater—the Grand—to see a stage show called *In Old Kentucky*.[27] It was his first Evansville theater experience, but it certainly was not to be the last. Since he found himself at a paper where "the staff was small and everyone became a jack of all trades,"[28] he had to produce line drawings to illustrate news stories and features in addition to cartoons. Interestingly, the "first staff political cartoonist on a national morning paper" in Great Britain was hired just two years earlier. This was William Kerridge Haselden, who played a significant role in making the *Daily Mirror* a success;[29] Knecht was to have a similar effect at the *Courier*. In 1933, Percy Carroll would say, "We engaged Karl Kae Knecht and I was always pleased, [as] no small part of the success of the *Courier* may be attributed to his cartoons. They are without a headache and good to the last drop."[30]

The first drop—Knecht's historic first cartoon for the *Courier*, published on September 29, 1906—showed an Evansville congressional candidate, John H.

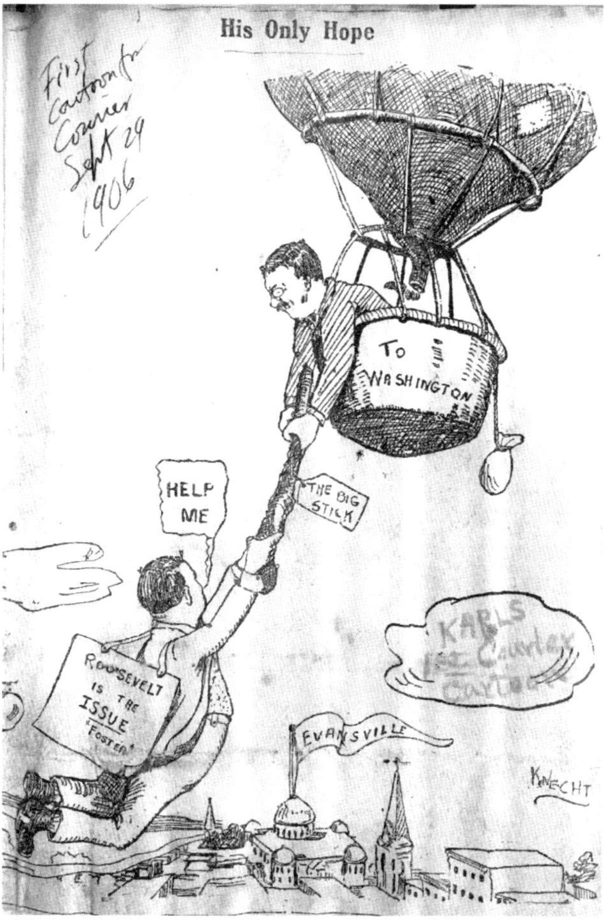

Knecht's first *Courier* cartoon, September 29, 1906. *UE.*

Foster, being pulled up by President Theodore Roosevelt's "big stick" into a hot air balloon labeled "To Washington." Given his own subsequent interest in flight, it is interesting that his first cartoon featured a flight over the city; in 1913, he became probably the first person in Evansville to fly in an airplane, and six years later, he was to take the first aerial photograph of the city.[31] This cartoon was the first of many Karl Kae Knecht cartoons to feature a caricature of a president, a politician who was "God's gift to cartoonists…with his toothy grin and macho exuberance."[32] It was also the first of many to display—albeit crudely—an aerial view of the city of Evansville. Captioned "His Only Hope," it was signed simply "Knecht."[33] Fascinatingly, unlike almost all of his eighteen thousand published cartoons, the original rough draft of this cartoon survives in the Archives at the University of Evansville. The four key components of the

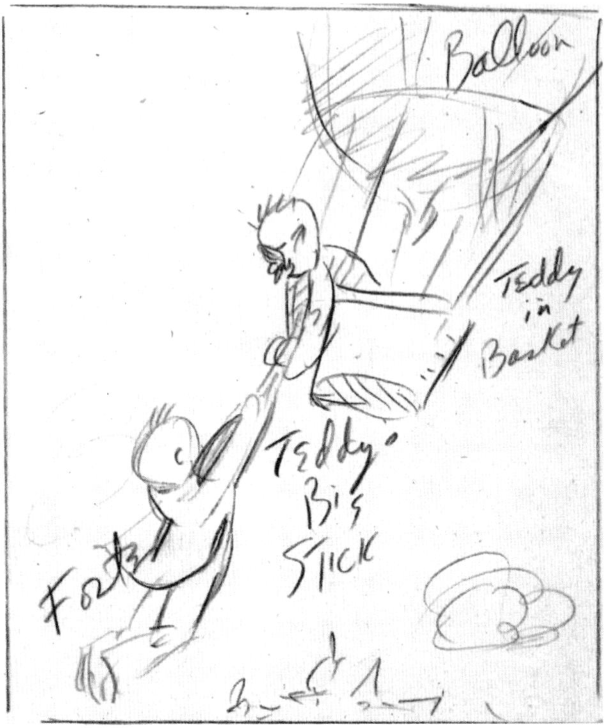

Knecht's first cartoon sketch, September 29, 1906. *UE/EVPL.*

eventual published cartoon are identified with simple labels: "Balloon," "Teddy in Basket," "Teddy's Big Stick" and "Foster." Knecht himself later labeled the drawing "My First One." As a start to his editorial cartooning career in Evansville, it was auspicious. In contrast to the printed cartoon, Knecht's rough sketch is fluid and vibrant, as almost all of his hand-drawn pieces were. The fact that there is a dynamic quality to the sketch that is missing in the published version is perhaps a result of the fact that for the newspaper version he was using the chalk plate technique.

Chalk plate was a laborious, old-fashioned and difficult technique with which Knecht was largely unfamiliar. Although he had seen his father use chalk plates, he had never used the method himself until he arrived in Evansville. It involved what amounted to engraving an image on "a baked solution of chalk and sodium silicate"[34] on a steel plate; this served as a mold from which a metal cast called a stereotype could be made, and as Charles William Hackleman said, "the quality and character of the results obtained in printing from stereotypes made from chalk plates depends entirely upon the artists' ability to sketch or engrave the design upon the plate."[35] The engraving was done with special steel tools, although Knecht once said, "I've used a hat pin when I was hard pressed."[36] Some fifty years later, he described the cartoon-making process in these early years with words so vivid that the reader can almost feel that they are looking over his shoulder at the dingy old *Courier* offices at 125–27 Main Street:

> *I would make my cartoon on copy paper, exact size, just a pencil dummy sketchy style. Get an o.k. or if "NO*Kay," submit others or use* [*Courier* editor Percy] *Carroll's idea—if suggested. Placing that over a "chalk plate" I would go over the lines with pencil, lightly. That would make a faint impression on chalk. Then with steel pointed "styluses"...of varied size points from fine one, ⅛ to ¼ inch or more. The chalk* [was] *about ¼ inch thick. I would then cut lines through chalk to steel base but not enough to scratch steel. Could cross-hatch, shade, etc. to heart's content, or with wide points make solids. Faint chalk left often gave crayon effect. Blowing chalk all the while. Had an ordinary apron. Later one like a dentist or MD uses with high neck and tied in back. Could not smoke as you worked...too much blowing. Results would surprise—lines sharp and clear. Rarely was a plate faulty—if so would break off in spots. I even patched some such with saliva and chalk dust. Finished, would take to the stereotypers. They warmed plate on edge of molten metal pot. Then placed it in casting box, just as they do matrix. Poured molten metal in and presto there was the metal cut.*[37]

There were not many newspapers still using this technique by 1906. Phil Ensley has said that Knecht was "one of the last to use chalk plate," and according to the distinguished historian of cartooning Richard E. Marschall, the printed cartoons that emerged from the chalk plate technique "were a confusion of awkward, angular lines." The *Courier* was to use chalk plates until about 1920.[38] Almost all of Karl Kae Knecht's early printed cartoons in the *Courier* look somewhat awkward and stiff, and it seems that although this might partly be explained by the roughness of a young artist's earliest work, at least some of the blame for that can be laid on the unfamiliar and challenging medium with which he was being asked to work. The artist himself acknowledged both aspects; a small handwritten note in the scrapbook of his early cartoons says by way of explanation, "These all on 'chalk plates.' Attribute some to crudeness."[39] And like all great artists, he mastered his craft. Twenty-five years later, former *Courier* co-owner H.C. Murphy observed, "With the passage of time...the K.K.K. creations adorning the first page became surer; as the artist's technique grew more

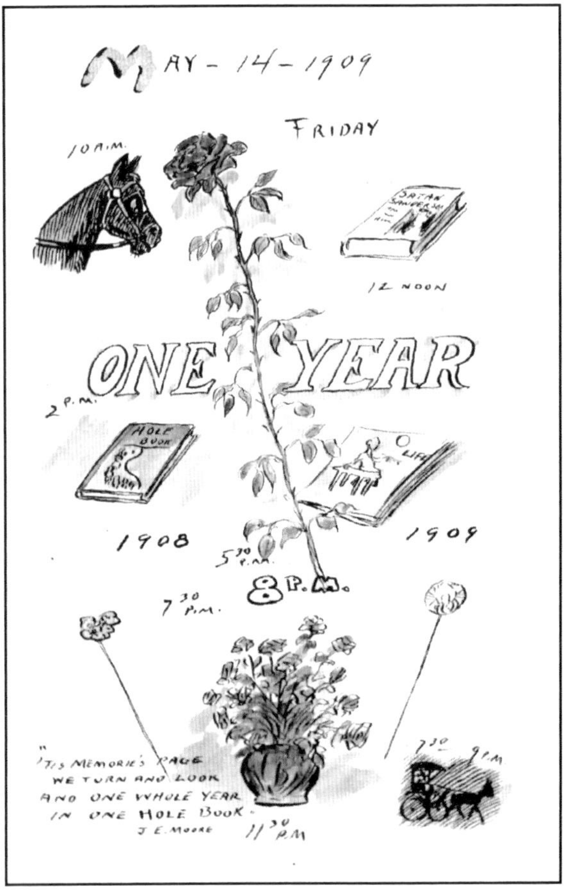

One of Knecht's hand-drawn journals, May 14, 1909. *University of Southern Indiana Archives (USI).*

perfect and his interpretation of significant local events became more acute and accurate."[40]

After two years in Evansville, Knecht met Jannie Ellwood Moore, and ten years later, they married; the marriage was to last until his death, fifty-four years later. They had met "after Mr. K peevishly cartooned Jannie and her friend the morning after they'd appeared at the Majestic Theater wearing the enormous picture hats that annoyed him so on lady show-goers."[41] Cartoons, clearly, can have powerful and presumably unintended consequences. Throughout 1909, Knecht kept an almost daily visual journal, each day marked by beautiful little hand-drawn and water-colored images, most of which revolve around his relationship with Jannie.[42] They got married on August 22, 1918, in a simple early morning ceremony at her parents' home that "was marked by the absence of music and attendants

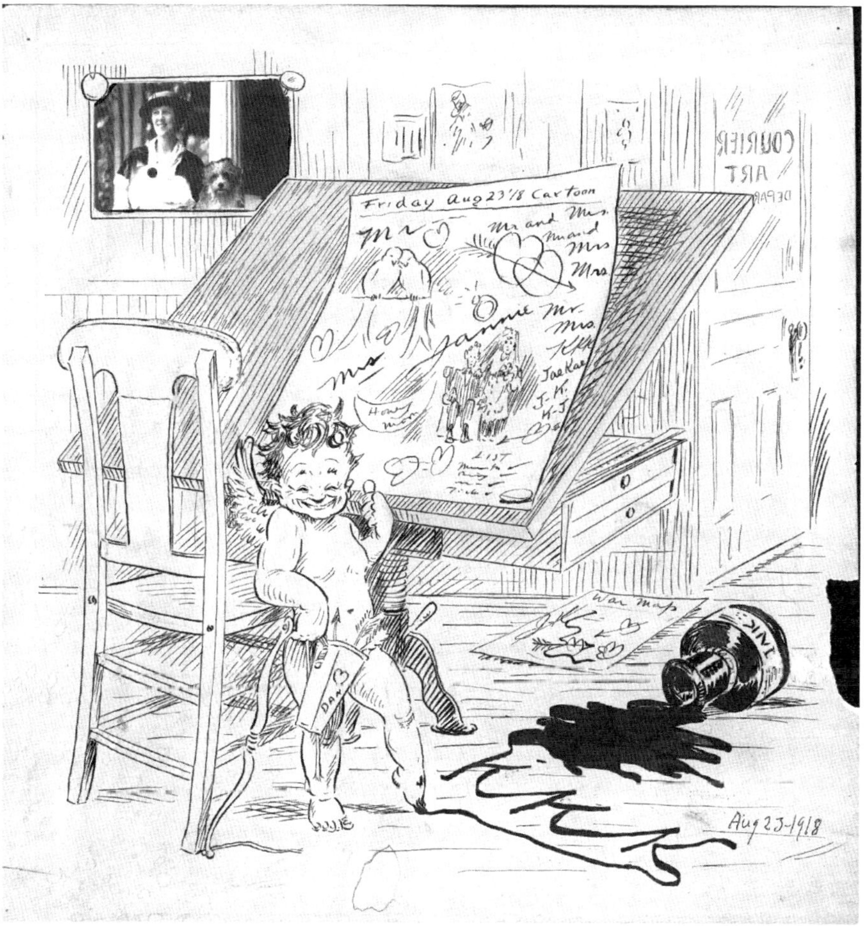

Cupid at Knecht's drawing desk the day after his wedding, August 23, 1918. *UE/EVPL.*

and the usual pomp and circumstance of weddings" and was attended only by their immediate families.[43] In a cartoon published the day after their wedding, he depicted Cupid at his *Courier* drawing desk, pointing to a series of sketches of hearts, arrows and lovebirds, with a little drawing of the couple on their wedding day. Pinned to the wall behind the desk is a real photo of Jannie and their dog. Phil Ensley believes that "it was her loyalty to family in Evansville that may have kept Karl here in spite of offers of better jobs elsewhere. If her happiness lay in being here, that was where he wanted to be; for him it was not a sacrifice."[44] Marie Horton Woods, who worked with Knecht for thirty-five years, said that of all his many interests, "the first of these was Jannie." She described her as "the lovely lady who has been his understanding companion, and his sweetheart across the years."[45] They lived at 31 Adams Avenue, in what is now called the Haynie's Corner Arts District. The couple had no children and were able to travel widely both in the United States and abroad. Jannie died in 1979 at the age of ninety.[46]

In 1908, he began taking his art on the road, with his immensely popular *Chalk Talks*; these shows—during which Knecht drew "funny pictures and cartoons with colored crayons"[47]—were a regular event around the tristate area until his materials were lost in the 1937 Evansville flood. He delivered these performances to numerous schools, organizations, businesses, churches and civic groups, including in 1918 to the Evansville Woman's Rotary Club; this was, said Knecht, "my first before an audience composed entirely of ladies." He described what the performance involved: "They put me right to work. I told them how cartoons are made and what wonderful men the cartoonists are and all that—and then I drew some pictures for them, patriotic and a number pertaining to ladies. They laughed and applauded and I guess I pleased for Miss Edythe Wells, the president, thanked me on behalf of the club. It was doubly kind of her for I had dared to sketch a caricature of her—the only local sketch."[48] In 1949, on a trip during which

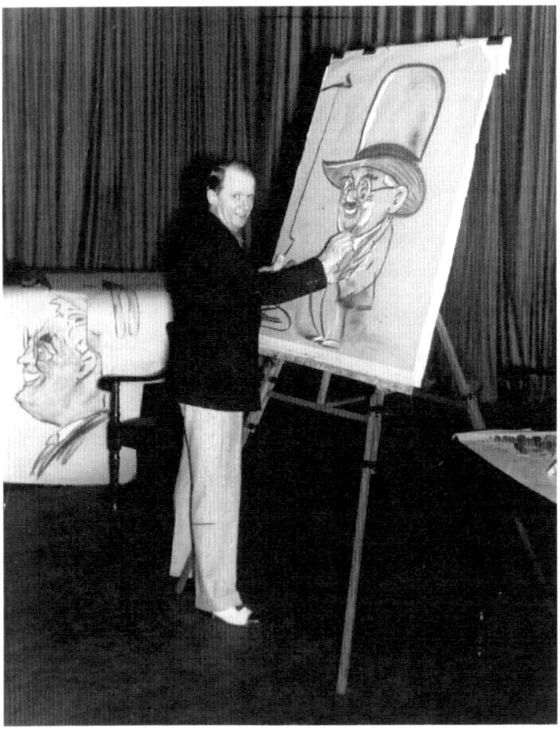

Knecht draws "Mr. Public" during one of his Chalk Talks, circa 1933. *Willard Library (WL).*

he met President Truman and sketched him in the Rose Garden of the White House, he delivered a *Chalk Talk* at the Library of Congress Auditorium in Washington, D.C.[49]

He resurrected the *Chalk Talks* to entertain healthy American soldiers in 1943 and injured servicemen in 1944, but this was far from his first effort on behalf of America's wounded warriors. He had performed *Chalk Talks* for the wounded during World War I, at the West Baden hospital near French Lick, at the Soldiers' and Sailors' Hospital at Boehne Camp and at the U.S. Marine Hospital in Evansville.[50] In 1918, he had launched an appeal for canes to help wounded men and had gathered over three hundred by December. As the *Courier* reported, "The wounded soldiers who are at the government hospital at West Baden, Ind., formerly the big hotel at the resort, are now hobbling about or walking over the pretty grounds swinging canes which the people of Evansville and nearby towns sent them through the appeal of *Courier*'s cartoonist K. K. Knecht."[51] The canes, which were "for the most part, good, heavy, substantial ones" and which sometimes came from prominent local families, were also later handed out as Christmas gifts to the wounded men.[52] During World War II, in addition to drawing over one thousand cartoons that certainly could be said to contribute to the war effort, he performed at the USO club at Eighth and Main Streets, in what was described as "one of the more popular of the Sunday evening entertainment series."[53] Strikingly, Knecht also delivered a *Chalk Talk* to the Lincoln USO, which in heavily segregated Evansville was located in the traditional black neighborhood and was for African American servicemen only.[54] The station hospital at Camp Breckenridge, Kentucky, witnessed a *Chalk Talk* for "ambulatory patients" in February 1944, and in October, he presented one at Camp Campbell, Kentucky, and another at the veteran's administration facility in Danville, Illinois, that was described as "a grand success."[55]

In 1910, Karl Kae Knecht created a figure to represent the common everyman—a figure called "Mr. Public" who, albeit with some evolution in terms of appearance, would go on to appear in hundreds of his cartoons. Bald, bespectacled and usually wearing a hat, he would become one of Knecht's most distinctive creations. Most of the time, he would represent Evansville, but he often stood in for a wider American population. He first appeared on March 1, 1910. It is particularly interesting because the person who often gets the credit for inventing such a cartoon everyman is Vaughn Shoemaker, who, according to the *New York Times*, was "an editorial cartoonist who created the character John Q. Public…[who] represented the beleaguered American taxpayer. The character appeared first in *The*

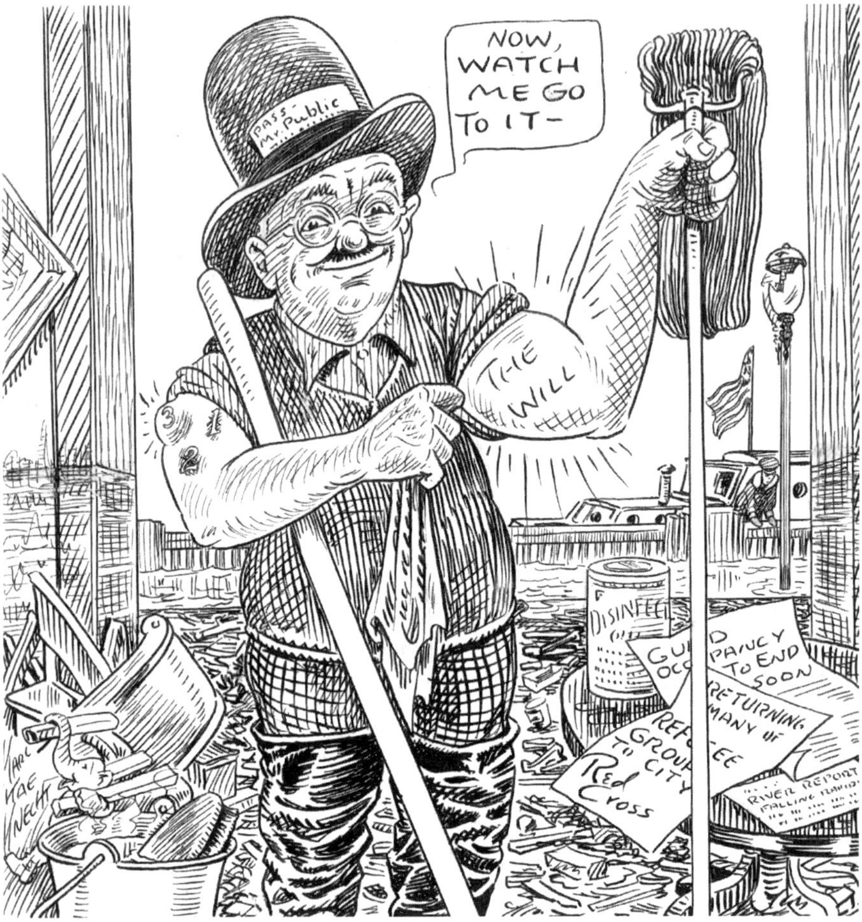

"Mr. Public" cleans up after the flood, February 10, 1937. *UE/EVPL.*

Chicago Daily News, the paper on which Mr. Shoemaker began his career in 1922."[56] In turn, Shoemaker was probably drawing on a character created in 1900 for the Hearst newspapers by Frederick Burr Opper called "Mr. Common People"—a "meek, little, puppet-like figure…a foolish, frightened, insignificant dwarf" forever oppressed and preyed upon by the greedy and the powerful.[57] What makes Knecht's Mr. Public distinctive is that while Opper and Shoemaker's figures were rather weak—"perennially suspended between bewilderment that their left pants pocket had been picked and dread that their right was about to go next"[58]—Knecht's was often a proactive and dynamic player. He plays an equal role with FDR and Uncle Sam in the first post–Pearl Harbor cartoon discussed earlier and in one of Knecht's most famous cartoons, published on February 10, 1937, he takes the lead in the battle to clean up the city after the devastating flood of 1937. Far from being weak, here Mr. Public displays his bulging biceps; he has "3…2…1" tattooed on one arm and "THE WILL" tattooed on the other. He holds two mops and boldly challenges the reader—into whose eyes he is looking directly—by saying, "Now, watch me go to it."

Knecht used his art to speak as an activist on behalf of a host of local causes, and it is hard to imagine that they could have had a more prominent advocate than the man whose cartoon appeared in the middle of the front page of the newspaper virtually every day from 1906 to 1952. Just to cite one representative example, he was a lifelong supporter of the American Red Cross from its earliest days in Evansville. "When the Evansville Chapter was established in 1917, Knecht drew 'Fall In,'…a cartoon emphasizing the need for Red Cross members. As the years passed, Knecht took an interest in the various services the Red Cross provided and published cartoons which helped increase emergency funding…Through his cartoons Knecht stressed what individuals could do to help the agency, and people reacted by giving to the Red Cross Relief Fund."[59] On his retirement in 1960, the executive director of the Evansville chapter said to him, "Your messages were always very impressive. Thank you for all the times you have told the Red Cross story."[60] His cartoons brought welcome attention—and funds—to local events, churches, clubs, organizations and causes both large and small.[61]

Between the two world wars, Knecht made two enormous contributions to the permanent shape of Evansville through his activism on behalf of the establishment of two of the great and enduring institutions of the city—the University of Evansville (then Evansville College) and Mesker Park Zoo. When Evansville was attempting to get a college in 1917—in fact to move an existing college from Moores Hill, Indiana, to Evansville—the key event was a remarkable public fundraising drive that raised $500,000 between April 15 and May 3.[62] Knecht threw his weight behind the campaign in an extraordinary way, drawing cartoons related to the campaign on thirteen successive days, from April 23 to May 5. It was almost certainly the most focused cartoon campaign on a single subject of his fifty-four-year career. The cartoons made a very powerful argument for the necessity of a college in the city—indeed, the first one, which showed the "kick-off" of the campaign, was starkly captioned "A Game We Must Win." Amusingly, the final cartoon in the series, after the dramatic but successful completion of the campaign, was entitled "Now Then—Back to Other Things" and showed a variety of other potential cartoon topics—"The War, The Garden, Baseball, Etc." ringing the doorbell

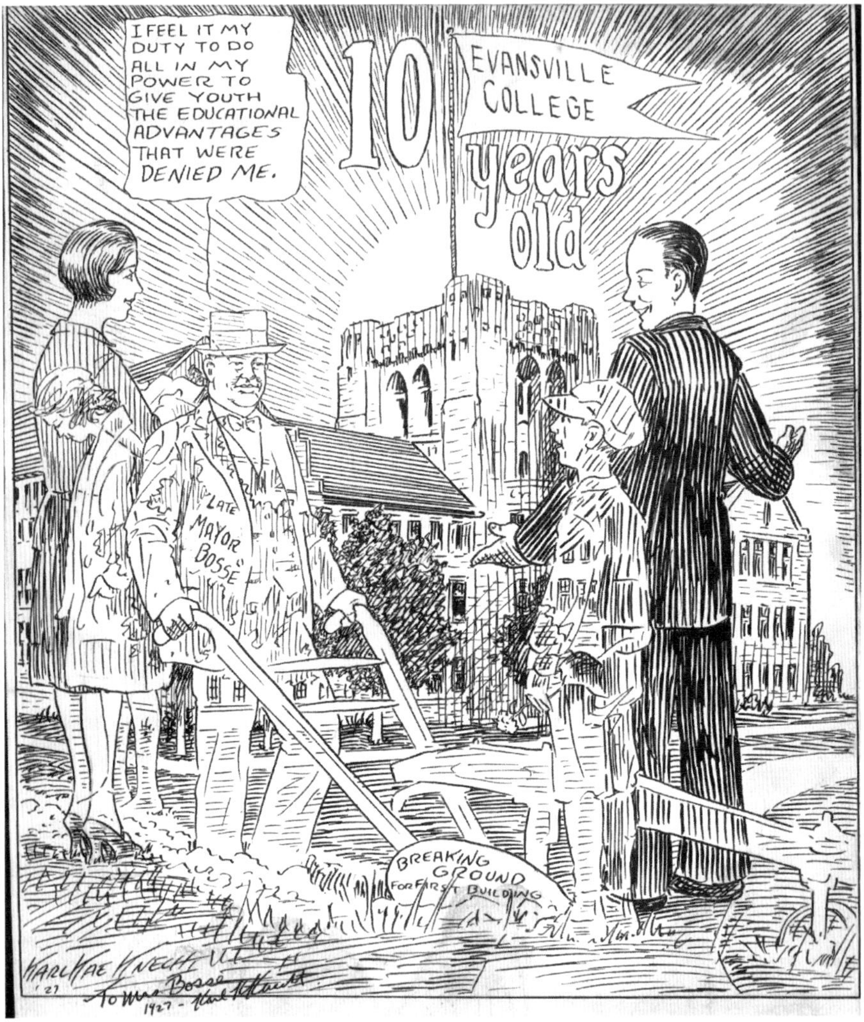

Ten years of Evansville College, 1927. *UE/EVPL.*

and waiting impatiently for a figure called "Evansville" to emerge from where he was admiring his new "College" mortarboard. It is, of course, impossible to quantify exactly how important a role Knecht's activism played in the successful execution of Evansville's most noteworthy fundraising effort—the biggest one before this was a mere $150,000—but it is fair to say that his cartoons communicated the message in the clearest way possible.[63] In 1953, the grateful college granted him an honorary doctorate, and in the citation, it was said that he had been "in the vanguard of that courageous group together

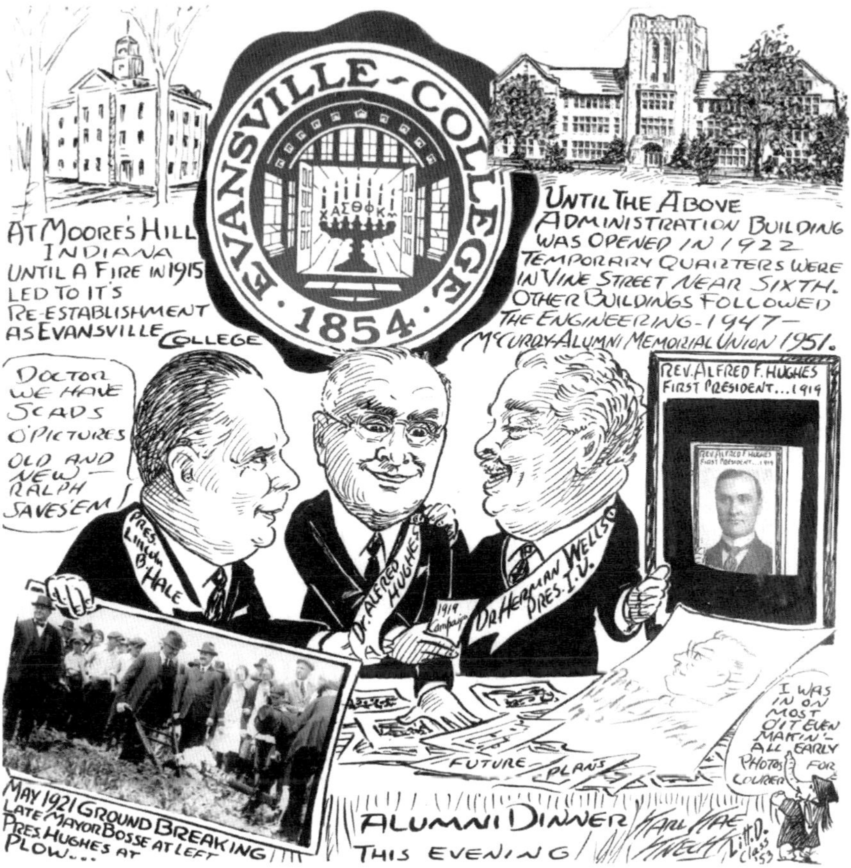

Centennial of Evansville College, 1954. *UE/EVPL.*

with George Clifford, Benjamin Bosse, Howard Roosa, Alfred F. Hughes and many others who had the vision to bring the College to Evansville."[64]

He continued to support Evansville College throughout his career, frequently drawing cartoons that drew attention to the institution and its affairs, including fundraising. A ghostly image of Benjamin Bosse adorns the cartoon that marked ten years of the college in Evansville in 1927. It shows Bosse working the plow that was used in the groundbreaking ceremony in 1919, based on the photograph of the same event taken by none other than Karl Kae Knecht. Bosse is uttering a version of the phrase with which he began the college fundraising campaign—"I feel it my duty to do all in my power to give youth the educational advantages that were denied to me." In 1954, Knecht marked the centennial of Evansville College—1854 was the year of the foundation of Moores Hill College—with a beautiful image that reflected not just the history but also his own connections. Interestingly, it actually includes one of the photographs that Knecht took at the groundbreaking. This one has President Alfred F. Hughes taking his turn at the ceremonial plow with Bosse a smiling figure to the left. Kay the elephant is wearing an Evansville College graduation cap and gown, and the cartoon is signed "Karl Kae Knecht Litt. D. Class '53." It is an interesting image in that it shows several of Knecht's traits: the use of photographs literally cut and pasted into the image; the use of older existing drawings (such as Evansville College's Administration Hall in the top right of the cartoon) similarly pasted in; his great skill as a caricature artist—much of his *Chalk Talk* notoriety was based on his uncanny ability to draw caricatures—and finally his great talent for drawing buildings.

If helping to bring a college to Evansville was not enough, ten years later Knecht almost single-handedly started Mesker Park Zoo. His significance in this regard is well illustrated by the fact that when the Evansville Zoological Society published a history of the zoo in 2011, the first chapter was simply entitled "Karl Kae Knecht."[65] One day in 1928, Knecht was offered two lions on the condition that they could be given appropriate accommodation. When he asked Mayor Herbert Males about it, the mayor responded, "Great! Get us the lions and we'll get the cage. Rest assured of that."[66] By April, the lions, Belle and Brutus, were in place, and Mesker Park Zoo was born. Brutus reportedly "roared out his gladness to be out of the shipping crate" on arrival.[67] Knecht "took a leading part in its growth and progress," and given his love of elephants, it was perhaps inevitable that he would want one for the zoo. He started a campaign to raise enough money to bring an elephant to Evansville.[68] He began the campaign on March 17, 1929, with these words, written in his own inimitable style:

> *Did you know that we are going to get an elephant for our City Zoo? That we, ourselves, are going to buy it, you and me? Well we are, all the children—young as well as old—no age limit at all—these but a day old or those one hundred years of age—all of us.... The elephant will then really belong to the children. When they grow to womanhood and manhood and perchance become mothers and fathers they can then take their children to the zoo and there point to the elephant, also that many years older, and tell how they helped to buy it.... Give or send whatever amount that you can, the more the better—your pennies, a nickel, a dime, quarter, a half or full dollar, or five, ten or even more dollars as so many have....* The Courier *and* The Journal *will print a list of the donations every day.*[69]

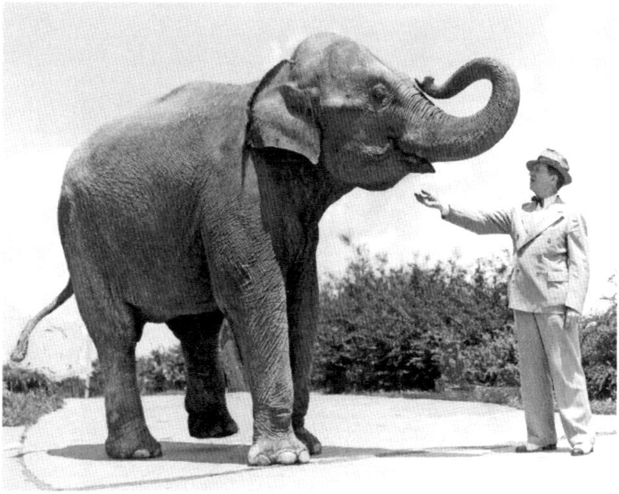

Karl Kae Knecht with Kay the elephant, 1930s. *WL.*

Contributions of all sizes poured in, and less than one month later, on April 9, the fund went past its goal with a gift of $1,500 from Mrs. George Mesker, who told Knecht in the letter containing her check that the gift was "inspired by the intense interest which [had] been shown" by the city's response to his appeal.[70] As a result, the zoo was able to purchase the single most significant animal that it ever had—a Burmese elephant that was named Kay after Karl Kae Knecht. As was said in one account of the history of the zoo, written in 1978, "For 25 years, life at Mesker Park Zoo revolved around Kay, who remains for many the keenest memory of the facility…[as she was] the biggest zoo attraction."[71] One of Knecht's most memorable cartoons was drawn for the day that Kay arrived at the zoo, June 14, 1929. Captioned "How Our City Appears Today," it is an aerial rendering of the city of Evansville, with the city drawn in the shape of an elephant. Kay's route to Mesker Park Zoo is shown as a procession of very cute little elephants, and at the zoo, a little boy and a little girl jump for joy on her arrival while Kay raises her trunk in salute.

It seems very clear that although others played significant roles, the existence of a zoo in the city can largely be attributed to the activism of Knecht. Looking back in 1990, the *Evansville Courier* said in an editorial, "Without the efforts of Karl Kae Knecht, Evansville might never have had a zoo. Indeed the creation of Mesker Park Zoo can be traced to the longtime *Courier* cartoonist…[Knecht] loved the zoo and his community loved him. And, for good reason, the zoo's first building was named for him."[72] He drew numerous cartoons related to the zoo, and of course, Kay the elephant was present in almost all his cartoons after 1928.

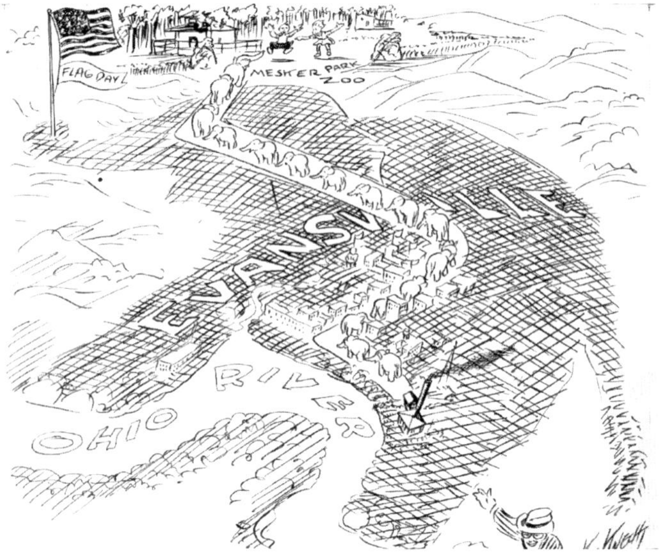

Kay comes to Mesker, the city shaped like an elephant, June 14, 1929. *UE/EVPL.*

Tragically, the real elephant Kay was to be involved in the death of two of her keepers; the first was Jack Mayer, a part-time zookeeper who died after an alleged interaction with her in 1938—although the precise role played by Kay was probably limited.[73] The second was the zoo's director, Roger "Bob" McGraw, who died of injuries he received from Kay in 1954.[74] Knecht's position was complicated, and he both drew a cartoon and wrote a column defending Kay and justifying her actions.[75] In immediate response to McGraw's death, though, Knecht drew one of his starkest and most powerful cartoons, a response to an elephant that he loved killing a man whom he admired. The cartoon shows a pair of robed female hands hanging up a wreath beside an elephant hook with "Bob McG" inscribed on it. The wreath has a ribbon wrapped around its bottom half on which is written "To R.F. 'Mac' McGraw, Kay's and all 300 animals [*sic*] friend. From his and their friends—the children of today and of yesteryears." It is a cartoon that emanates deep regret and great sadness, a formidable response to an event that undoubtedly traumatized him.

Shortly after his successful quest to bring Kay to Evansville, and long before the tragic dénouement to that story, Knecht was fêted in celebration of his fiftieth birthday, in 1933. It was also considered his twenty-fifth anniversary of working at the newspaper. During this event, described as "the biggest surprise of his life," some remarkable tributes were paid to him—all the more notable when it is remembered that he was not yet even half way through his tenure with the *Courier*.[76] The tributes reflected how highly he was thought of, and although they ranged from the serious to the comical, they all communicated

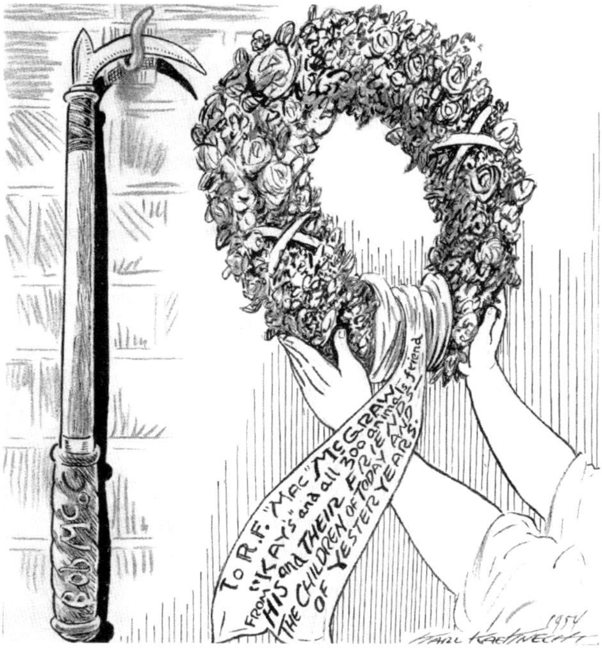

The death of "Bob" McGraw, February 1954. *UE/EVPL.*

the level of esteem at which he was held, all across the country. A telegram from the White House said, "Twenty-five years of faithful service to the newspaper public and fifty years of honorable living deserve the recognition Evansville gives to him. Mighty as is the pen used by the writing fraternity, the drawing pen as used by Mr. Knecht is a power unto itself. I feel sure the President would send a congratulatory message to Mr. Knecht if he were here."[77] Howard Roosa, one of the giants of Evansville life in the twentieth century and a former owner and editor of the *Courier*, said this:

> *For twenty-five years we of the former and present* Courier *staff have looked up to him as our guide, philosopher and friend but we had no idea what a doddering old bird he was. Association with this sweet and genial spirit has been an inspiration for all of us younger men. The reproduction of his cartoons in books and magazines made us proud that we were* Courier *men.…For twenty-five years the brilliant cartoons of Karl K Knecht have influenced the thought of the* Courier's *great and enlarging clientele. More than that, their graciousness, their luminous qualities, their fairness, even in the heat of battle, have moulded* [sic] *the character of thousands of* Courier *readers. The people of the Tri-state territory are finer in texture, more mellow in their outlook on life because of the great cartoons appearing from day to day by the great cartoonist.*[78]

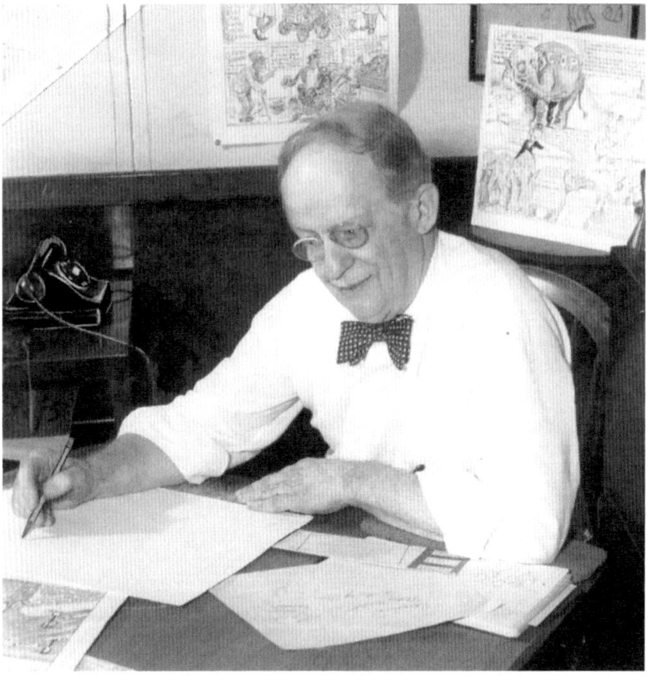

Karl Kae Knecht at work, 1951. *WL.*

Elmer Noelting, a senior executive with the Faultless Caster Company, called him the "assistant director of thought along higher planes in this community," and Leslie Eichel, a former editor of the *Evansville Press* who was then with the Central Press Association of New York, said, "When I deal with many cartoonists, I strive to have them impart to their work that same quality which caused me in much younger days to await the Knecht cartoons so eagerly."[79] The brilliant cast of cartoonists at the *Chicago Tribune* sent a message that reflected both their respect and their sense of humor: "We have seen your stuff and think it's swell. Why don't you make a life work of it? To wish you congratulations we can't because there's not a cartoonist here who can spell it. Best of luck, cartooner. By the way you haven't got a spare idea we could use have you?"[80] The most highly paid actor in Hollywood, the humorist Will Rogers, wrote, "To my dear companion in public misinformation. Mr. Knecht there is nothing in the whole of news that has the power that a cartoon has. One cartoon is worth ten editorials and one half cartoon is worth 20 Rogers' gags."[81] Knecht himself would have appreciated the comment that came from the nationally syndicated columnist O.O. McIntyre: "To have worked on one newspaper for twenty-five years means one of two things: Mr. Knecht is an amazingly gifted cartoonist or has something on the publisher."[82] Perhaps the greatest tribute came from his boss—then *Courier* editor Don Scism:

When that work is prominently displayed on page one of a newspaper day in and day out for 25 years in the form of art whose reader-interest is exceedingly high, then we know that Karl Knecht's contribution to the character of The Courier *has been a tremendous one. In the case of Karl the man transcends the art. And the art is of a high quality. Karl is not only a good artist, a man of originality and imagination, but he has remained an unspoiled human being. He is what he is. That was true 25 years ago and it is true today. The years have not made of him a mere piece of an orthodox, and often dull, pattern of life that may be covered in a glib classification. He retains the challenging spirit of youth as well as its enthusiasms and forthright honesty of mind.*[83]

No discussion of his life would be complete with mentioning that Knecht was also a lifelong aficionado of the theater and the circus. From his first experience of a circus in Freeport at the age of seven, he was infatuated. In 1925, he started an organization called the Circus Fans of America and served in various capacities for that group over the years. He began, edited, wrote and drew for their magazine, entitled *The White Tops*, which was a "publication devoted entirely to circus work."[84] Syndicated columnist O.O. McIntyre called

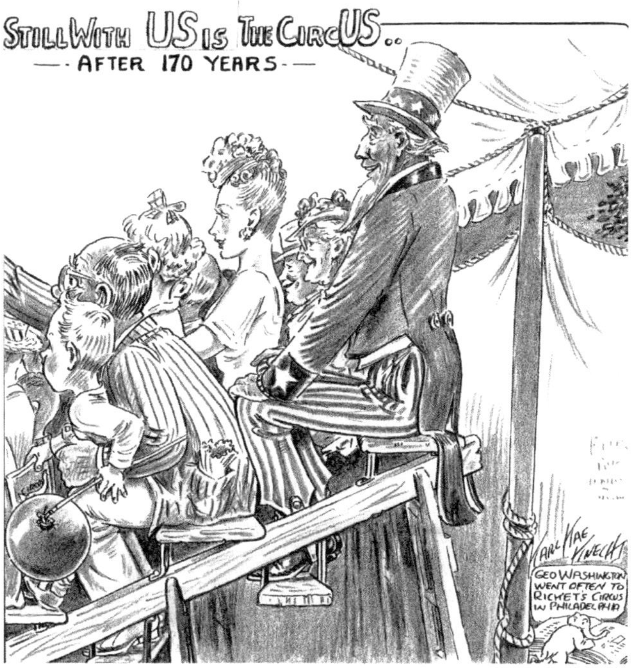

Uncle Sam at the circus, 1946. *UE/EVPL.*

him "the most enthusiastic circus fan in America."[85] Knecht wrote frequently about circuses and drew numerous cartoons that dealt with the subject. In one fine example from 1946, he celebrated 170 years of the circus in America with an excited Uncle Sam joining an enthralled Mr. Public and a variety of men, women and children of all ages sitting rapt in the Big Top. Kay observes, "Geo Washington went often to Ricket's Circus in Philadelphia."

He was also a huge fan of the theater, with this also dating back to childhood. As Phil Ensley said:

> *Karl's interest in show business increased when he attended the Columbia Exposition in Chicago in 1893, where he saw Buffalo Bill, Mark Twain, and Eddie Foy. He earned tickets for theatrical shows by passing out handbills, and by distributing programs and drinking water. This interest in the entertainment world continued throughout his career on* The Courier *and as correspondent for "Variety" and columnist for "Billboard."*[86]

As noted earlier, he spent his very first night in Evansville at the theater, and he wrote a column in the *Courier* for many years that was entitled, among other things, "Say Kay. What of Shows, Theaters an' Such!" And of course, he drew many cartoons that featured the theater and those who strode on the stage. His Sunday cartoon—called "Going and Coming" for decades, although it had some other monikers, too—was almost always a collection of small fascinating cameos about many different topics, and it

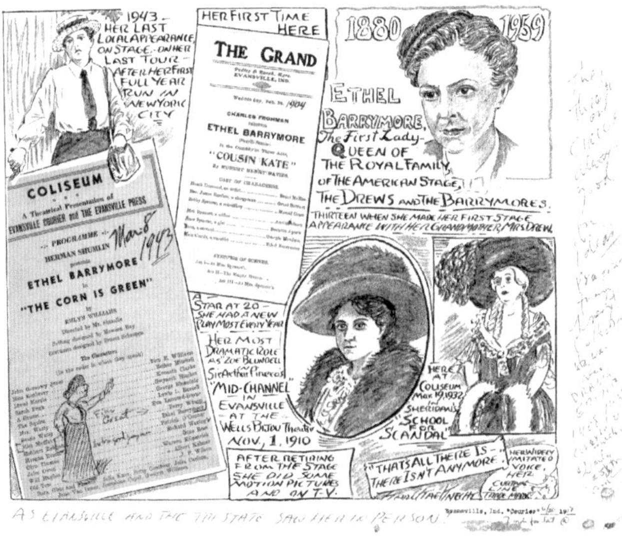

Ethel Barrymore, June 20, 1959. *UE/EVPL.*

frequently included something theatrical. His cartoon from June 20, 1959, is a celebration of the life of the actress Ethel Barrymore, who had died that year. A wonderful example of Knecht's work, it contains four drawings of Barrymore, a wealth of historical information and two actual artifacts pasted in. One of them even has a rough Knecht sketch on the front. Fascinatingly, there is a marginal note that says, "The theater and circus always good for ideas." Knecht's life and work were certainly proof of that.

In 1956, the *Courier* marked the fiftieth anniversary of Knecht's arrival at the paper with a cartoon on the front page (which no longer routinely carried them) drawn by Grover Page of the *Louisville Courier-Journal*. Entitled "An Elephant Never Forgets," it showed Knecht riding on the trunk of an elephant, carrying a pencil shaped like an elephant hook. The paper reflected on what had happened since his first day on the job:

> *Many things have changed since that day in late September of 1906.* The Courier *has expanded into a metropolitan newspaper, and Evansville is no longer a small city. Four editors have come and gone, a fifth is on the job since Knecht etched on a "chalk plate" his first cartoon for the Tri-State's largest newspaper. But Knecht—whose KKK-signed drawings have become a durable landmark to folks over much of three states—still is* The Courier*'s cartoonist. His sketched "editorials" still have the sting of old, and still they convey his love for the city he adopted as "home" so many years ago. The love and respect is not a one-sided affair.*[87]

The editorial page that day stated that his cartoons had "become as much a part of the Tri-State morning as the breakfast coffee," and that seems to be a fair analysis. Administrations changed nationally and locally, the paper was bought and sold, world wars came and went, fashions and music and popular culture changed with each decade, but Karl Kae Knecht was there virtually every day, drawing his cartoons. "A cartoonist," said the editorial, "can be a potent force in shaping public opinion and community thinking—and Karl Kae Knecht has compounded this influence during every one of his fifty years with *The Courier*. His work has been a blending of craftsmanship and good citizenship, spiced by a gentle, yet penetrating humor and tempered [by] the sound philosophy of a wholesome life."[88] Fine words to mark a very rare professional milestone.

The final professional milestone was the finishing post, as just four years later Karl Kae Knecht retired. Declaring that it was "time for less arduous pursuits," he submitted his last cartoon and walked away on June 1, 1960.

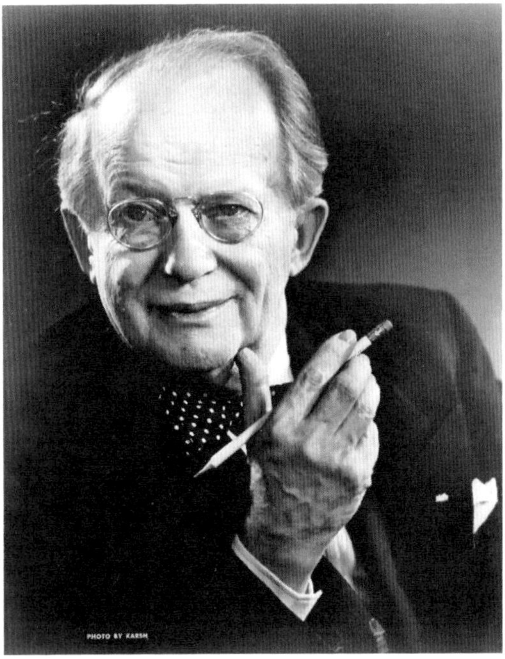

Karl Kae Knecht toward the end of his career. *WL.*

The last cartoon was captioned "—And With This, We Crawl Out From Under" and depicted Knecht emerging from under his artist's desk, to which was stuck a note saying "For Sale! (Museum Piece). Drawing Board Used by K.K.K. at *Courier* Since 1906." He reflected on his life of cartooning, and on retirement, with these striking words: "The consciousness of having to have a new cartoon idea every day is always prevalent during one's waking hours. Not to have to keep that in mind in all that one reads, hears, sees, and even dreams will be a relief."[89] "Few men," said *Courier* editor Earl E. Shaw, "are given an opportunity such as that enjoyed by Karl to be a force for good in the community in which they live."[90] Few men, of any generation, seized that opportunity with as much activist vigor as did Karl Kae Knecht.

Chapter 2

Racial Stereotypes in the Cartoons of Karl Kae Knecht

One of the hardest issues to discuss in the art of Karl Kae Knecht is his use of racist stereotypes, but it would be disingenuous to analyze his cartoons without acknowledging their presence. It is also important to make the distinction between his using racist stereotypes in cartoons and being racist himself. As will be seen, he drew powerful images against the Ku Klux Klan. He also spoke out against lynching and he supported the 1957 Civil Rights Bill, the first civil rights legislation since the nineteenth century. As has been seen, he performed at the African American USO during World War II, when Evansville was still rigidly segregated. In 1914, he delivered a *Chalk Talk* at the Liberty Baptist Church, and according to the *Courier*, "The entertainment is to be under the auspices of the colored YMCA, and from all indications Knecht will have a representative audience of colored folks." His long 1934 review of an all African American stage show called *Green Pastures* contained not a hint of racism.[91] In a segregated and routinely racist environment, there is no evidence to suggest that Knecht acted in a racist manner toward the people of color whom he encountered.

African Americans increasingly moved to Evansville after the Civil War, and they were heavily concentrated in one neighborhood of the city. By the end of the century, "about 50 percent of the new arrivals settled around Eighth and Canal streets and Lincoln Avenue, an area that came to be known as Baptist Town. Living conditions there were poor—some of the shacks were hardly habitable. Drinking water came from uncovered cisterns, there were open privies in backyards, and rats scurried in and out of garbage heaps. The mortality rate was high."[92] This slum area was cleared and a public housing project called Lincoln

Gardens was erected between 1936 and 1938—174 buildings were demolished on a thirteen-acre site.[93] The project was carried out as part of the New Deal by the Public Works Administration at a cost of over $800,000 and provided 191 living units in 16 buildings.[94] One indication of the level of institutional racism that Evansville's black population encountered can be found in a front-page *Courier* story on October 7, 1906—nine days into Knecht's tenure with the paper. The front-page headline is about a series of lynchings and attempted lynchings in locations ranging from Bloomington, Indiana, to Basin, Mississippi. The story describes in detail one that took place near Mobile, Alabama, and there is not a single word of condemnation for the people who carried out the lynching. In fact, the paper calmly says, "The crimes committed [by the lynched men]… were revenged by a party of forty-five men this afternoon.…Robinson, who committed the first crime that startled the people of Mobile and worked them up into a fury was first strung up."[95] The next day's paper carried a further five front-page stories related to lynch mobs, again without any critical comment.

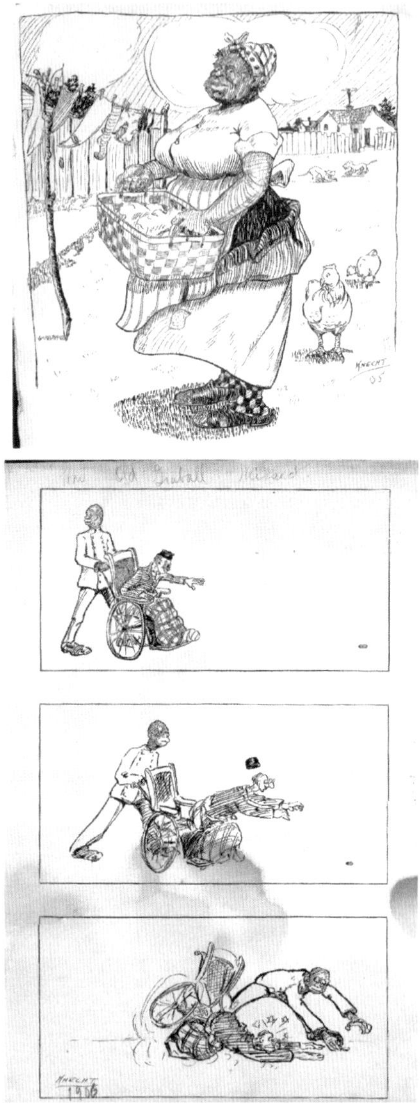

Racist images from Art Institute of Chicago, 1905–6. *UE/EVPL.*

There can be no denying that racist images appear in Knecht's work, especially in the early years in his depictions of African Americans and, during World War II, in his depiction of the Japanese. As early as 1905–6, in his Art Institute of Chicago drawings, there is clear evidence of the employment of racist tropes and stereotypes. Astonishingly, two of his first five cartoons

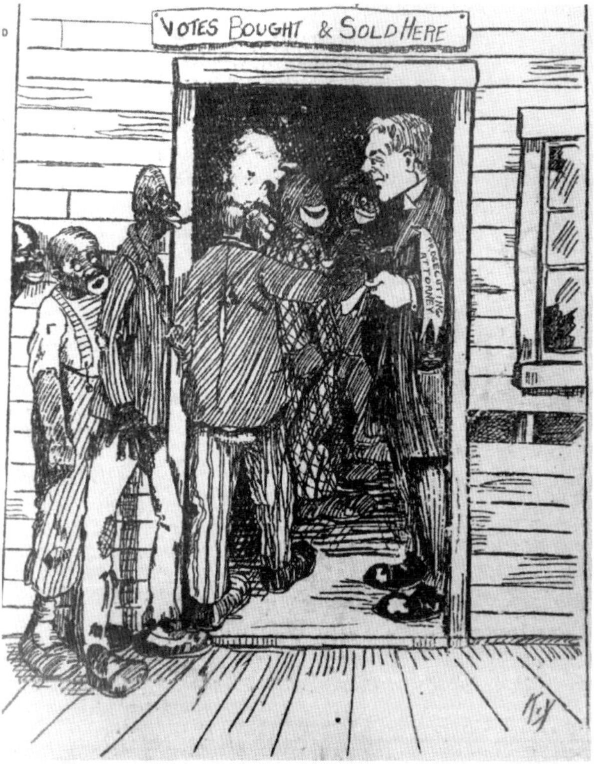

"A Shameful Spectacle," October 2, 1906. *UE.*

for the *Courier*, and five of the first twenty-seven, involve racist depictions of black people. "You Know What You Eat" on October 1 is bad enough, but "A Shameful Spectacle," published on October 2, is even worse. In just the fifth cartoon he drew for his Evansville audience, Knecht depicts six African Americans in a manner that is itself "a shameful spectacle"—so stereotyped and crude that the cartoon is hard to look at. His October 24 depiction of prisoners captioned "If You Were Sheriff" is just as deeply disturbing, as is the cartoon that appeared the following day with the same caption. All these images largely speak for themselves. So, too, do the drawings from his 1909 notebooks, which, with the addition of very unsubtle color and crude rendering of African American speech patterns, seem, if anything, to be even worse.

It did not end there. In 1937, he drew a cartoon that dealt with the construction of the Lincoln Gardens area. The Blue Goose that he references was a tavern in Baptist Town, at Governor and Douglas Streets, once called a "notorious dive" and "disreputable negro joint"; according to the *Courier*, "The Blue Goose is not only the worst saloon in Evansville. It is in all probability the toughest dive in the state."[96] This cartoon is undeniably

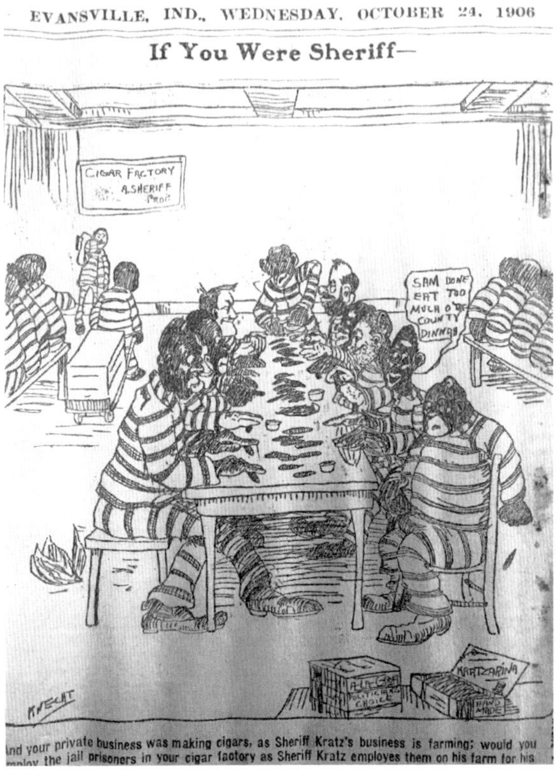

"If You Were Sheriff," October 24, 1906. *UE.*

racist in its depiction of African American stereotypes; stereotypical language, postures and facial features abound, and many of the tropes that he deployed thirty years earlier are still there.

All of these drawings by Knecht fit very much the definition offered by the historian Roger Fischer: "The genre was grandly racist: caricatures replete with grossly exaggerated lips, huge splayed feet, and kinky hair; tortured dialect imitative of minstrelsy; and situational satire that sank…low."[97] The images seem close to the clichés of blackface minstrelsy, "the most popular form of entertainment in the United States in the 19th century,"[98] and are very clearly part of a staggeringly universal cultural depiction of African Americans that Joseph Boskin summed up as "Sambo":

> *In journals, weeklies, newspapers, magazines, travel reports, diaries, brochures, and broadsides, there was Sambo, cited for his antics. His style filled the literary field in novels, short stories, children's tales, dime novels, essays, pamphlets, and leaflets. Visually, Sambo appeared in posters, on sheet music covers, post-cards, wooden pegboards, in illustrations,*

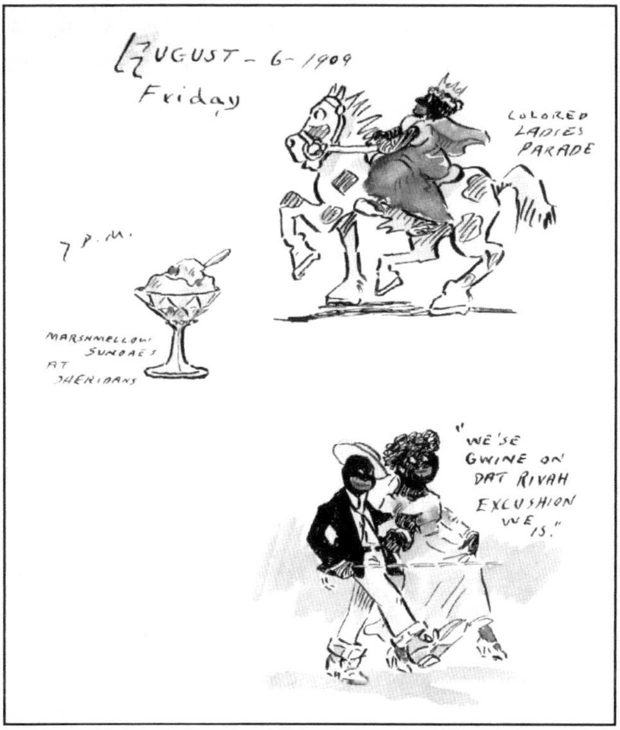

Racist images in Knecht's notebook, August 6, 1909. *USI.*

> *paintings, cartoons, comic strips, children's games, on postage stamps, in advertisements, on magazine covers, playing cards.... The material culture was full of him.... It was a testament to his ubiquitous talents that no part of the culture went untouched.*[99]

Knecht read a variety of weekly magazines—such as *Puck* and *Judge*—that at the turn of the century regularly ran such drawings of "Sambo," and it is hard to imagine that such racist norms did not bleed into his consciousness as a cartoonist. It would have been the path of least resistance, and it is also fair to say that cartoonists deal in oversimplifications and stereotypes every day. The problem for a white cartoonist using stereotypes while drawing black people, however, is that race becomes the center of the story. In the words of Ruth Thibodeau: "The very human characteristics drawn upon by the cartoonist to portray any individual, regardless of race, are also likely at times to have strong associations with a particular group, such as blacks. For the white cartoonist wishing to portray blacks in nonracist ways, these tenacious associations are bound to be problematic...[and] the possibility of the cartoon assuming a racist tone, at least in the eyes of some viewers,

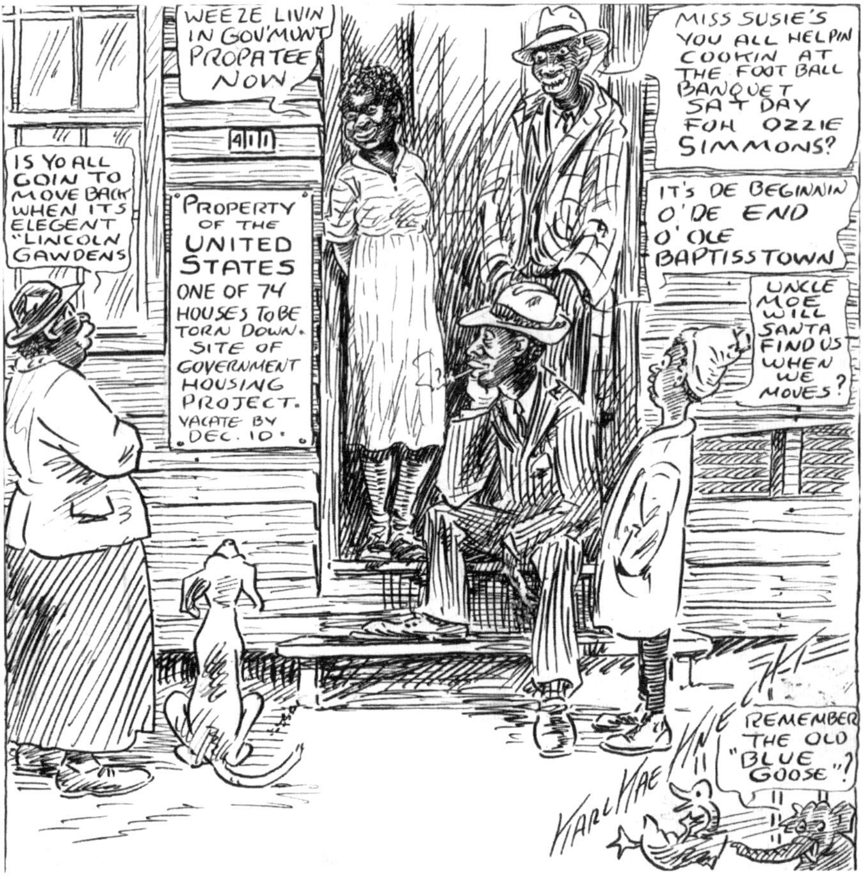

Lincoln Gardens to be built, 1937. *UE/EVPL.*

becomes even more probable."[100] Whether the "racist tone" in the cartoons of Karl Kae Knecht is a result of conscious or unconscious racism is hard—indeed impossible—to say, of course, but it reflects a pattern, one that is ultimately damaging. In the words of Roger Fischer, "However benign the intentions of reception of such ethnic caricature, it surely helped create and reinforce over the course of a generation an indelible impression that the droll darky…[was]—by dint of congenital shortcomings of intellect, culture, or character—forever barred from membership in the American family."[101]

The second area of "ethnic caricature" employed by Knecht was very specific to time and situation—it was his portrayal of Japanese people during World War II. The four sample Japanese faces shown on page 47 are almost breathtakingly racist to modern eyes, but they are a very fair representation of his routine

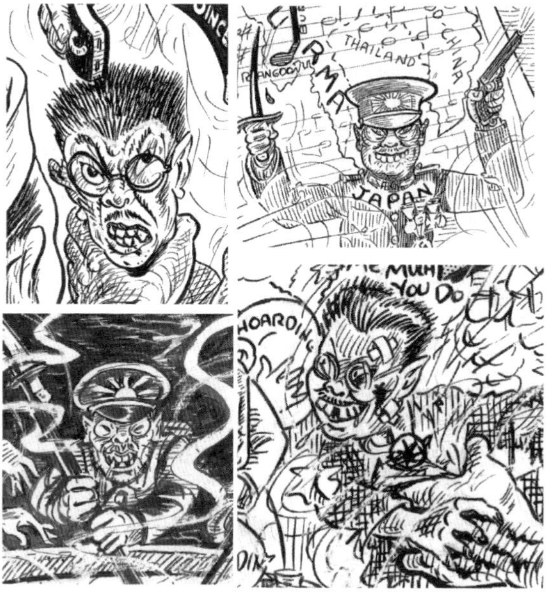

Four racist images of Japanese people from World War II. *UE/EVPL.*

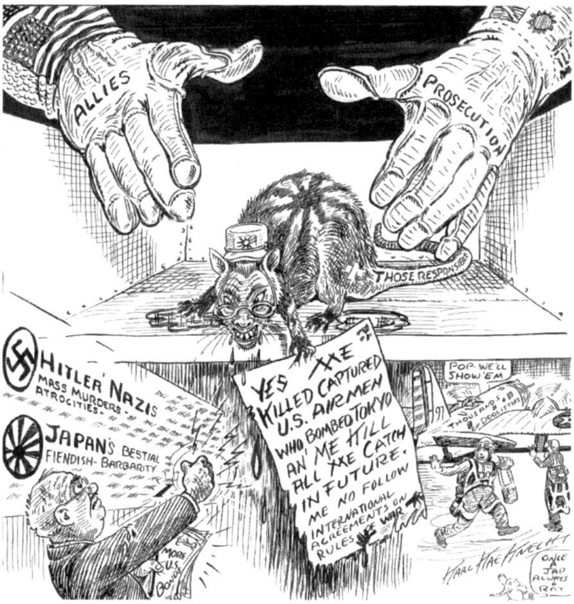

The Japanese depicted as a rat, April 24, 1943. UE/*EVPL.*

portrayal. His April 24, 1943 cartoon represents the Japanese as a rat and has Kay saying, "Once a Jap always a Rat." Knecht's September 20, 1944 cartoon depicts the Japanese as an unidentifiable creature swinging in the trees, but the caption reveals it to be an ape—"It'll Be Harder to Catch an Ape in the Trees Than Out in the Open." This book could quite literally have been filled with such racist images from this period—of the scores of images Knecht drew of the Japanese during the war, virtually every single one evidenced racial stereotyping.

It is easy—and justified—to call out the racism evident in these cartoons, but it must also be said that Knecht is working in a context where such things were commonplace and absolutely unremarkable. The immensely popular Admiral Bill Halsey, "a national figure" as the U.S. Navy's commander of the Third Fleet, could speak in the following

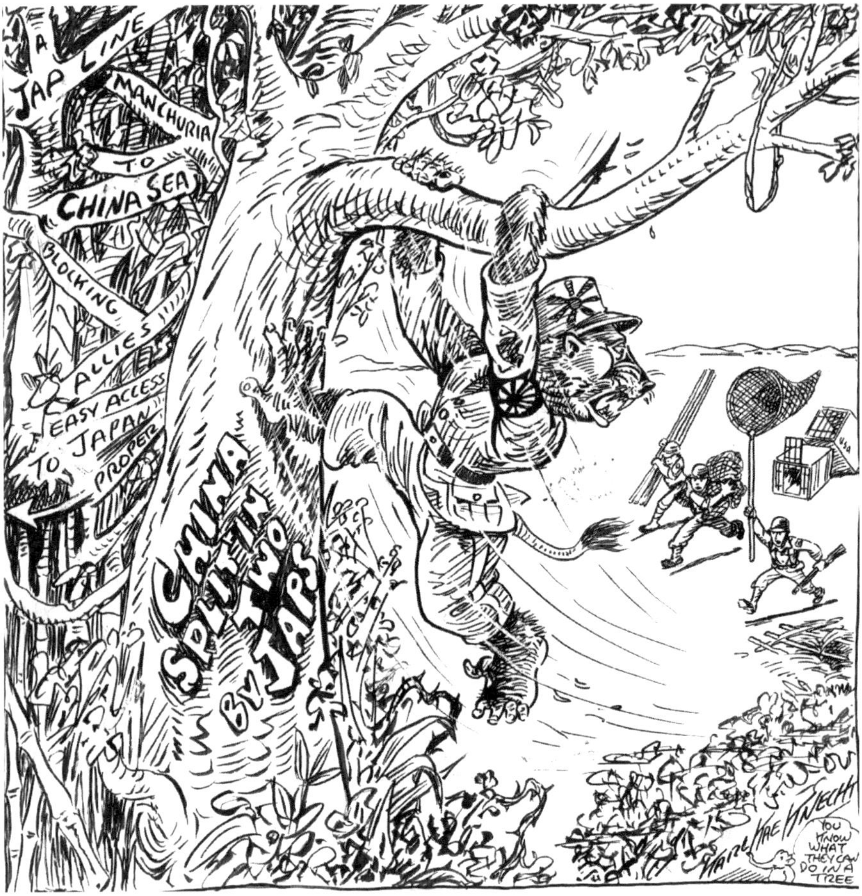

The Japanese depicted as an ape, September 20, 1944. UE/*EVPL.*

terms: "He began early in the war referring to the Japanese as 'rats.' 'Kill Japs, they're rats,' he often said. As the war progressed they became 'bastards' for a while, and then he switched to 'monkeys.' Finally, by war's end, the Japanese had become to Halsey 'lousy yellow rat monkey bastards.'"[102] For influential columnist Walter Winchell, "the Japs are savages," and Representative John Rankin of Mississippi referred to them—in the congressional record—as "savage apes" and in an *Evansville Press* story as "these brutal apes."[103] In 1945, Admiral Halsey was quoted in the *Evansville Press* (without comment or criticism) saying that he believed that "the Japanese race" originated from sexual intercourse between men and apes.[104] Even Hoosier everyman Ernie Pyle, whose columns ran in the *Evansville Press*, said, "The Japanese were looked upon as something subhuman and repulsive."[105] Such words translated into action. Japanese bodies were mutilated by American servicemen—ears, teeth, hands, bones and even skulls were taken as trophies, and as recently as 2015, there was at least one garishly decorated Japanese trophy skull residing in Evansville.[106]

Knecht's cartoons clearly fit into this environment, in which the Japanese were dehumanized and consistently presented as savages, rats and apes. As a cartoonist, he was most definitely not alone, and this racist dehumanization was propagated by some of the most famous names in cartoon history. Herblock, arguably America's greatest cartoonist of the twentieth century, depicted the Japanese as squinting, grinning and bucktoothed in a comment on the Sino-Japanese war of 1937.[107] Theodore Geisel, better known to generations of children as Dr. Seuss, drew "scurrilous" anti-Japanese cartoons in which he portrayed them as, among other things, alley cats and an organ grinder's monkey. This being Dr. Seuss, there are also various creatures of uncertain provenance, including something that looks like an orangutan with elongated crustacean claws wearing a topcoat and top hat.[108] Arthur Szyk, one of the most talented cartoonists of the century, "sank to racist stereotypes when describing the Japanese leadership….The Japanese, as was the case with Seuss and others, simply fit racial stereotypes."[109] The great David Low drew the "Jap" as a monkey swinging by its tail in two well-known cartoons entitled "East or West?" and "Strain on the Tail" and drew on a host of ethnic stereotypes in a cartoon called "Japanese balancing act," and the brilliant Leslie Illingworth drew Tojo as a bucktoothed and bespectacled monkey looking ridiculous in an ill-fitting governor's hat and coat.[110] Britain's most prominent cartoon magazine, *Punch*, published a famous cartoon in January 1942 of Japanese apes swinging through the jungle.[111] And ShiPu Wang has spoken recently of the "many racist representations in the print media that targeted U.S. residents of Japanese descent. These images often featured a similar monolithic representation of Japanese features: squat face, round-rimmed glasses, squinty eyes, and grimacing buckteeth that in some posters look like those of vampires."[112] That description applies perfectly to virtually every single example of Knecht's portrayal of Japanese people during the war.

In conclusion, there is no escaping the fact that Karl Kae Knecht drew many cartoons that contain racist imagery. There is also no escape from the fact that the United States in this era was a fundamentally racist country—as were many others—and that he was a product of the times in which he lived. While there is no evidence that he was himself a racist, the uncomfortable racist images that he leaves behind are a powerful and sobering reminder of the country and the world that he spent his life documenting.

Chapter 3

A Very Brief History of the Editorial Cartoon

Most leaders consider the cartoon's ability to undermine political legitimacy a genuine threat. Consequently, the history of the political cartoon is shadowed by attempts to silence their artists. Both Aristotle and Aristophanes describe the torture of a cartoonist named Pauson for his attack on Greek leadership. French artist Honoré Daumier was sentenced to jail for his satirical derision of King Louis Philippe and the aristocracy. Adolf Hitler ordered that the name of English cartoonist David Low be put on the Gestapo's list of people to be exterminated. More recently, Kurdish cartoonist Dogan Guzal was sentenced to 16 months in high-security prison in August 1998 for depicting his government as weak. One of the most famous silencing of a political cartoonist was the assassination of Naji Ali in 1987 for his criticism of Arab and Palestinian leaders.[113]

Like the remarks of Victor Navasky quoted earlier, these words of Ilan Danjoux from 2007 make it clear to us that cartooning is no joke. Cartoons have helped to change the world, and activist cartoonists have earned plaudits and awards; however, their efforts have also brought them criticism, censorship, torture, incarceration and even death.[114] In January 2015, this message was made manifest when the *Charlie Hebdo* offices in Paris were attacked and five cartoonists were murdered.[115] Many would argue that the existence of cartoons is a sign of a healthy society. The Venezuelan cartoonist Rayma Suprani once said, "Cartoons are a thermometer for a country's freedoms,"[116] and this is true both at a national and a local level. In order to fully understand Karl Kae Knecht, then, it is vital to understand that what he was doing was engaging in a profoundly serious endeavor, one that has been in existence for thousands of years.

The first cartoonist was probably a caveman mocking his adversaries by daubing on a cave wall, although this is admittedly hard to prove. Karl Kae Knecht, himself keenly interested in the history of the genre, argued in 1940 that "cartoons were a means of expression before man learned to express his thoughts in the form of printed or written symbols…when man expressed himself in crude drawings on cave walls."[117] It seems likely the first one that can be authenticated, albeit with some questions, is the artist who produced an image of the Egyptian pharaoh Akhnaton well over three thousand years ago; there are many other examples on Egyptian sarcophagi, monuments and gravesites.[118] The Chinese, the Greeks and the Romans certainly left many examples, and in Europe during the Middle Ages, images that look a lot like cartoons adorned both books and buildings. Medieval cathedrals, for example, often have carved comic and grotesque elements, such as gargoyles; the eleventh-century Lincoln Cathedral's spectacular Judgment Porch features a cartoon face on the devil's private parts while elsewhere in the cathedral resides the famous Lincoln Imp, a "grinning imp…carved in a seated position with one leg crossed over the other."[119] It is hard to quantify how many generations of Lincoln Cathedral congregations have giggled with delight on first encountering these visual treasures.

The religious conflicts of the sixteenth century were when images that look like modern cartoons really began to emerge. Sheri Klein has said, "All humour has the power to disrupt our expectations and associations in both subtle and obvious ways." This certainly seems to have been the case when Protestant Reformers like Martin Luther and their supporters used shocking visual images to disrupt the way people thought about the Roman Catholic Church, with the church responding in the same way. "Satire mocks art and life with more of a bite than parody," said Klein. "The aim of satire is to prompt us to re-examine our values, social behaviours and morals. The visual satirist uses the knowledge of the behaviour and conventions of a culture or group to mimic and magnify the ridiculous, as found in caricatures."[120] Woodcuts, posters and broadsheets proliferated, featuring grotesque representations of ecclesiastical opponents that mimicked and magnified their faults and failings, real and imagined; the effect of such visuals must have been great on what was a largely illiterate audience. Luther, "keenly aware of the persuasive power of pictures,"[121] worked with a friend, the artist Lucas Cranach, who once drew the pope as the Whore of Babylon from the New Testament Book of Revelation and, on another occasion, depicted the pope being excreted by the devil.[122] Erhard Schön's *The Devil with Bagpipes* was another striking piece of Protestant cartoon polemic, showing the devil playing a monk as if he were a bagpipe; it is much reproduced and much misinterpreted.[123]

Drawings that were "delightfully bawdy and scandalously irreverent" and that are recognizably cartoons had certainly emerged by the eighteenth century, especially in England.[124] Some of the most important were created by William Hogarth (1697–1764), an artist who "not only felt the pulse of his age, he quickened it."[125] In the first part of the century, he produced a series of prints that were both amusing and fiercely critical of the social realities of the London in which he lived and worked, "satires on the follies and vices of the age,"[126] such as *Gin Lane* from 1751. The ability to be both simultaneously extremely serious and very funny seems like a modern phenomenon—like *The Daily Show* or *The Colbert Report*—and yet this duality was an essential component of Hogarth's genius. Harry Mount said of Hogarth's socially critical prints in 2014, "These days, though, you look at those morality tales and you don't feel chastened—you smile. The reason why Hogarth's name lives on is not thanks to his moralising, but because of his wit, and his skill at capturing the British character at its bawdy, drunken, pleasure-loving best and worst."[127] Mount is not quite correct, however; almost three hundred years later, these images retain the power to both shock and amuse.

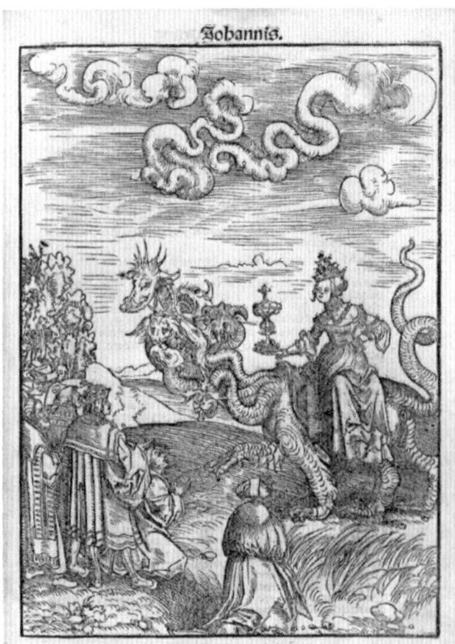

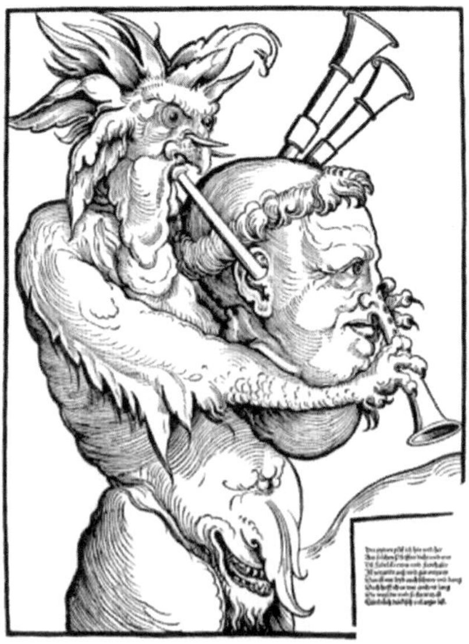

Left: The pope is depicted as the Whore of Babylon by Lucas Cranach, 1545; *right*: The devil is depicted playing a monk as bagpipes by Erhard Schön, circa 1530. *Public domain.*

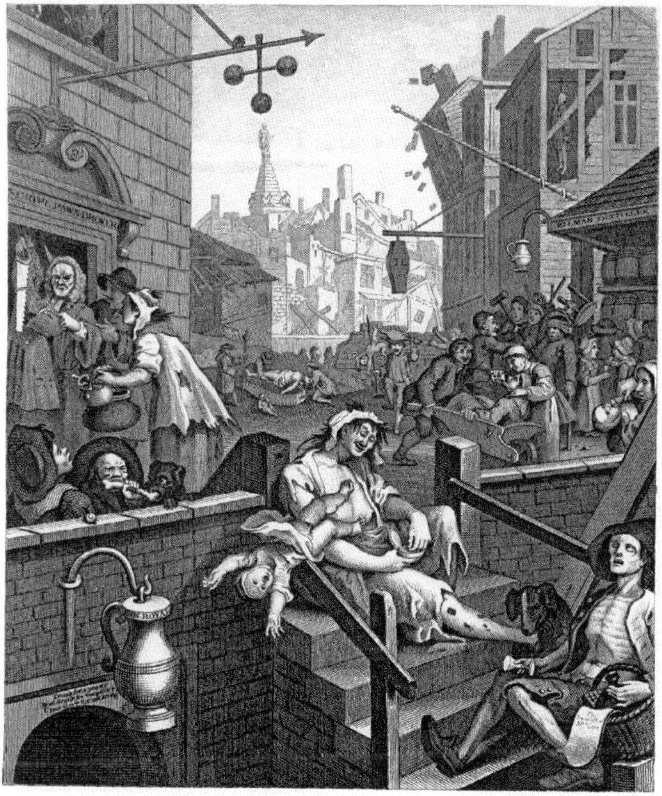

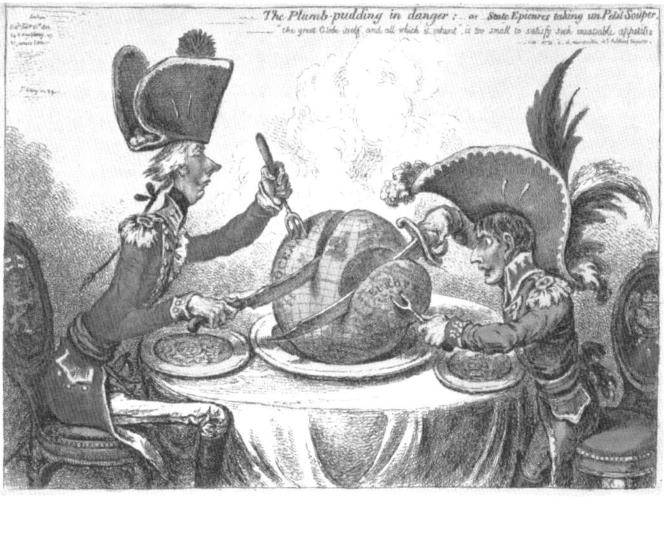

Top: William Hogarth, *Gin Lane*, 1751; *bottom*: James Gillray, *The Plumb Pudding in Danger*, 1805. *Public domain.*

Hogarth died in 1764, and in many ways, the next generation of great English cartoonists form the bridge from the early modern to the modern age of cartooning. James Gillray (1756–1815) also lived in London, where he lived with a publisher and print seller, Hannah Humphrey: "Three decades before cartoons could be served up in newspapers or magazines with any ease or practicality, they supplied an enthusiastic upper-class public with a steady diet of pungent political satire, both political and social."[128] He savagely attacked the royal family, especially King George III, as well as both French and British politicians. His 1805 picture of British prime minister Pitt and French leader Napoleon Bonaparte carving up the world, *The Plumb Pudding in Danger*, is one of the most influential cartoons ever drawn. Martin Rowson's comment on the lasting effect of these two cartoonists is apt:

> *To a large extent we understand the 18th century through Hogarth and Gillray's eyes. From a world before photography, it's Hogarth's vision of London that has endured, with the savage slapstick of its greater and meaner thoroughfares, its strutting rakes, syphilitic whores, gin-sodden murderers, squashed cats and gallows. Likewise, if we have a visual awareness of Britain's statesmen from the tail end of that century, it's probably Gillray's versions of them: the freckly beanpole Pitt or the spherical Charles James Fox.*[129]

Stylistically, they have had a profound influence. In the words of Martin Rowson on another occasion, "The standard template for political cartoons—the caricaturing of real people into an alternative, shape-shifted reality, where they act out a narrative of the cartoonist's devising—was concreted in by Gillray 230 years ago and has remained completely unchanged ever since."[130]

Thomas Rowlandson (1756/7–1827), influenced by Hogarth and an almost exact contemporary of Gillray, has been credited with creating the first real cartoon character ("Dr. Syntax") and being the first to consistently use speech balloons and horizontal strips of boxed images—the "two stock conventions of the strip cartoon."[131] His work was less political, and less moralizing, than those of Gillray and Hogarth—according to Amelia Rauser, rather than offering political solutions or social criticism, he merely portrayed Georgian society "with bemused detachment." That is not to say his work was not unsettling; his "Dinners Drest in the Neatest Manner" from 1811, for example, is easily one of the most grotesque and disgusting depictions of food preparation ever created.[132]

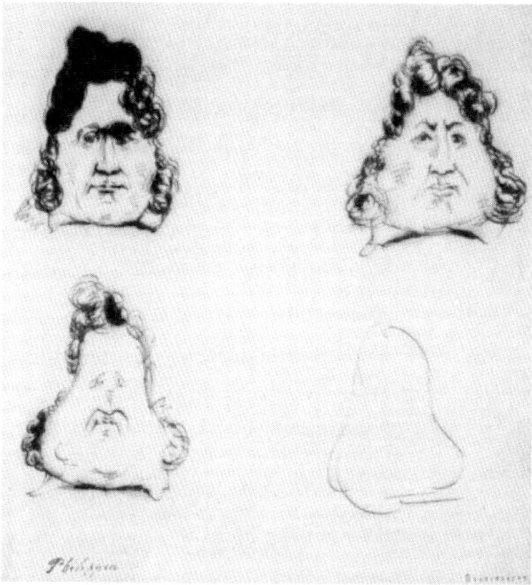

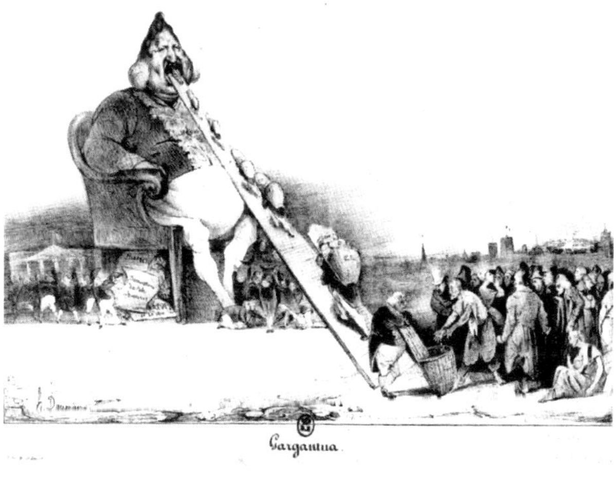

Top: Charles Philipon's depiction of the French King as a Pear Face, 1831–32; *bottom*: Honoré Daumier's "Gargantua" from 1832. *Public domain.*

George Cruikshank (1792–1878) is the last of this remarkable set of savage British cartoonists; he knew Gillray, inherited his art table and even finished some of his uncompleted pieces.[133] His brilliant work was both political and social, weighing in on contemporary party politics but also contributing to the cause of abstinence from alcohol. He might be best known for this temperance campaigning or as an illustrator of the works of Charles Dickens, but his political images are still extremely powerful. He famously depicted Prime Minister William Pitt as "A Toadstool Upon a Dung-hill" in 1791, and in 1819, he produced the astonishing "Poor Bull and His Burden," a "vitriolic satire on taxation, militarism, and civil and ecclesiastical corruption," depicting a bleeding and muzzled British bull crushed by a hierarchy consisting of tax collectors, politicians, the military, the judiciary, the church, royal courtiers and, at the very top, the Crown.[134] In many ways, it is a cartoon that resonates with today's political critiques from both left and right, with its powerful condemnation of entitled and interconnected elites oppressing a noble but silenced majority. Cruikshank is also notable because his work sometimes appeared not just as prints but also in pamphlets, where his political images appeared alongside political writing—"the direct precursors of Philipon's Parisian journals." The story now moves to Paris; after 1830, "the cartoon centre of gravity shifted from England to France." And at the center of all that were Charles Philipon and Honoré Daumier.[135]

Philipon (1800–1861) founded the magazine *La Caricature* in 1830 and employed a stable of satirical artists. They went after many targets, but most famously, they attacked the political corruption of the day, with their animus centered on the king, Louis-Philippe. In the words of David Kerr, Philipon "cultivated a network of talented artists who worked almost exclusively for him and who, under his leadership, waged an unprecedented and relentless war of attrition against Louis-Philippe and the July Monarchy [with] [t]he corrosive wit of their intensely violent imagery."[136] Philipon is most well known for his rendering of the King's (admittedly pear-shaped) head as a pear—the French word for pear also having the alternate meaning of "fathead." On being prosecuted, he famously produced a series of drawings in court in which the king's head gradually, almost imperceptibly, became a pear, and he asked, "Can I help it if His Majesty's face is like a pear?" He was prosecuted multiple times, fined heavily and sentenced to a year in prison.[137] Of all the cartoonists who worked with Philipon, by far the most influential was Honoré Daumier (1808–1879)—"one of the greatest social critics that ever held a brush"[138]—and of all his artworks, by far the most infamous is *Gargantua* from 1832, which depicts the king, massive, repulsive and bloated, sitting on a commode. He "defecates rewards to the tiny ministers of his government gathered beneath the chair. Other ministers collect tribute from the destitute and crippled populace of Paris and then march up a gangplank to feed the baskets of wealth to the ravenous king. The king's body—obese, passive and immobilized by gluttony—is the agent of his own physical corruption." Daumier was arrested, prosecuted, convicted and imprisoned.[139]

What is seen with all of these artists over the years is a willingness to be fiercely critical of those in authority, a commitment and loyalty to the place

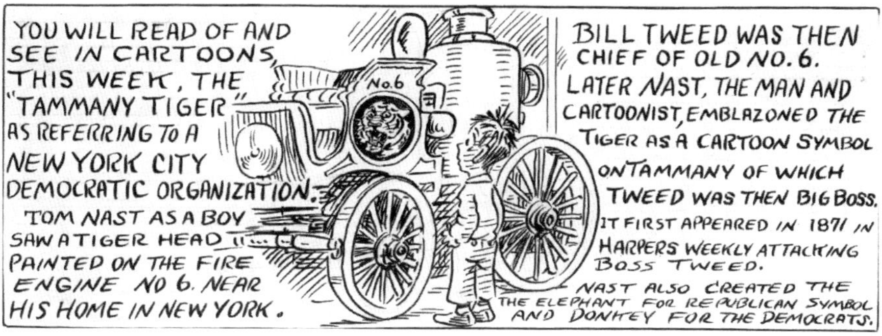

Young Thomas Nast, undated. *UE/EVPL.*

they called home, a powerful imagination married to artistic talent and a willingness to take risks to make a social or political point. All of this is seen in the work of Thomas Nast (1840–1902), the "father of American political cartooning."[140] According to Karl Kae Knecht, "Nast was the first to use many characters in use today, such as the donkey for the Democratic Party, the elephant for the Republican Party, a goose for socialism, the square cap which cartoonists use on 'labor,' and the roly-poly Santa Claus."[141] He was also a man willing to use savage satire to take on William "Boss" Tweed and the entrenched power brokers of Tammany Hall in New York in the early 1870s. His cartoons, which appeared in *Harper's Weekly*, lambasted Tweed and his gang and eventually destroyed their political power; in arguably the most famous line ever uttered about political cartoons, Tweed said, "Let's stop them damned pictures. I don't care so much what the papers write about me—my constituents can't read; but damn it, they can see the pictures."[142]

Thomas Nast died in 1902, the year that Karl Kae Knecht graduated high school. Knecht drew a cartoon of Nast as a boy and called him "the pioneer of all the newspaper editorial cartoonists."[143] He clearly greatly respected Nast's contribution to the profession, and as a historian of cartooning, Knecht was well aware that what he himself was doing was building on a foundation that had been laid by artists over the past centuries. Little did he know that his own name would one day be added to the annals of the cartooning profession, and it is to Knecht's life's work—the cartoons—that this book will now turn.

Chapter 4

CARTOONS 1903–39

Karl Kae Knecht began his studies at the Art Institute of Chicago in 1903, and his professional life as a cartoonist in Evansville began in 1906. Between that time and 1939, he drew thousands of cartoons on numerous topics, and he covered some of the most momentous events of the century, including World War I, Prohibition, the Great Depression, the growth of aviation and the sinking of the *Titanic*. He also covered one of the most significant stories in the history of Evansville—the great flood of 1937—not just as a cartoonist but also as a pioneering photographer. This chapter will examine some of the most striking cartoons from this first period of his professional life.

The first cartoons in this section are wonderful examples of Knecht's ability as an artist and are included here even though some of them are not strictly cartoons at all. His undated drawing of Abraham Lincoln, *The Young Man of 21 in 1830*, is believed to be part of his output while at the Art Institute of Chicago between 1903 and 1906. Although a rough sketch, perhaps unfinished, it is nevertheless fascinating. It contains many of the essential ingredients of the Lincoln boyhood myth—the axe, the split lumber, the log cabin and the book, in this case a book of law. Although a man of action and strength, he is also a man of contemplation and perhaps even vision, as he seems to be deep in thought and looking to an as-yet-unknown future. It is reminiscent of two very famous later works: *Lincoln the Rail Splitter* by J.L.G. Ferris (1909) and Norman Rockwell's 1965 painting of the same name. The contemplative element is also present in Indiana sculptor E.M. Viquesney's *Lincoln as an Indiana Boy*,

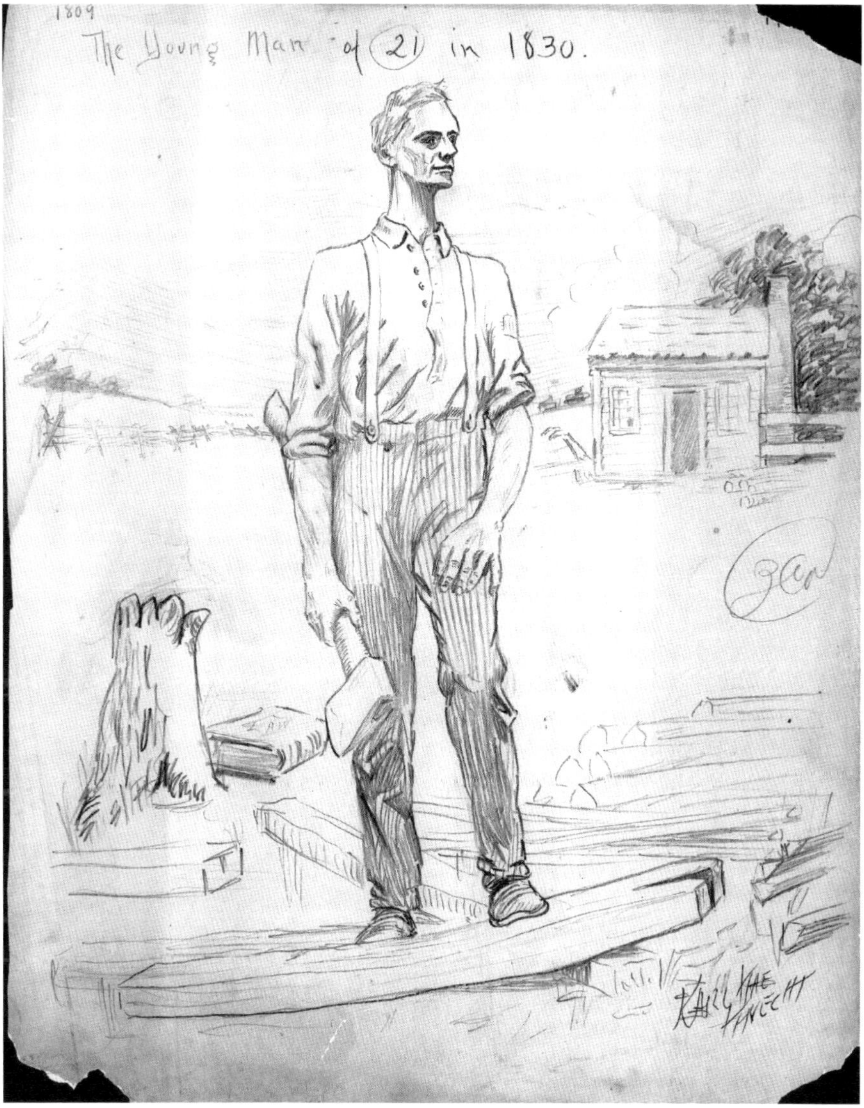

Young Abe Lincoln, circa 1903–6. *UE/EVPL.*

produced in 1938.[144] Another of Knecht's Art Institute drawings—a female nude from 1905—is included simply to give a sense of his accomplishment as an artist. Smooth and realistic, replete with depth and feeling, it reminds the reader that an ability to draw well lay at the heart of his success, although he said in 1947, "In a cartoon the idea is the main thing. Next in importance is the composition of the drawing. Third, comes the drawing."[145]

Three other cartoons produced between 1912 and 1932 offer further evidence of his profound technical abilities as an artist, although the first is a clear example of what is a moral gray area for any creative person: plagiarism. It is a striking image of a herald bringing in the baby New Year 1912 while the old year departs; the herald wears the livery of the *Evansville Courier*, and the cartoon was drawn for a special edition of the newspaper—it did not appear in the standard January 1 edition. Knecht added "with regards to Partridge" under his signature, a common practice when one cartoonist imitates or produces a pastiche of another work of art. In the words of Martha H. Kennedy:

> *Creators of comic art frequently borrow, adapt, or transform elements of artistic traditions or prototypes they deem useful for their projects....As part of the creative process, cartoonists also reference genres, artistic modes, and classic prototypes well recognized within the field of comic art itself. Some examples play on or off a specific drawing or predecessor's or peer's creative contribution and can be seen as a tribute to or respectful acknowledgment of the originator.*[146]

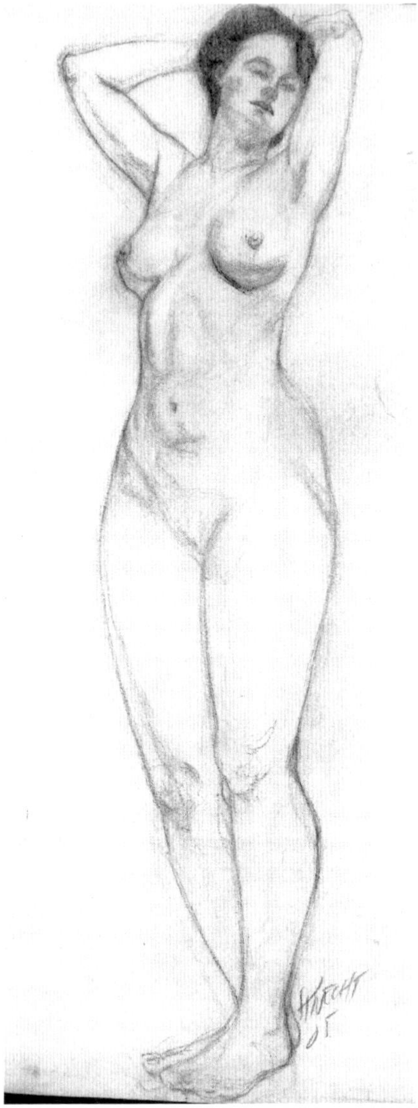

Full-length portrait of a female nude, 1905. *UE/EVPL.*

This one, however, is pushing this convention to the absolute limit. Sir John Bernard Partridge (1861–1945) was one of Britain's most influential cartoonists, drawing for *Punch* for over half a century. He also drew cartoons for commercial companies' advertising, including Selfridge's department stores, and in 1909, he drew an opening-day advertisement for that

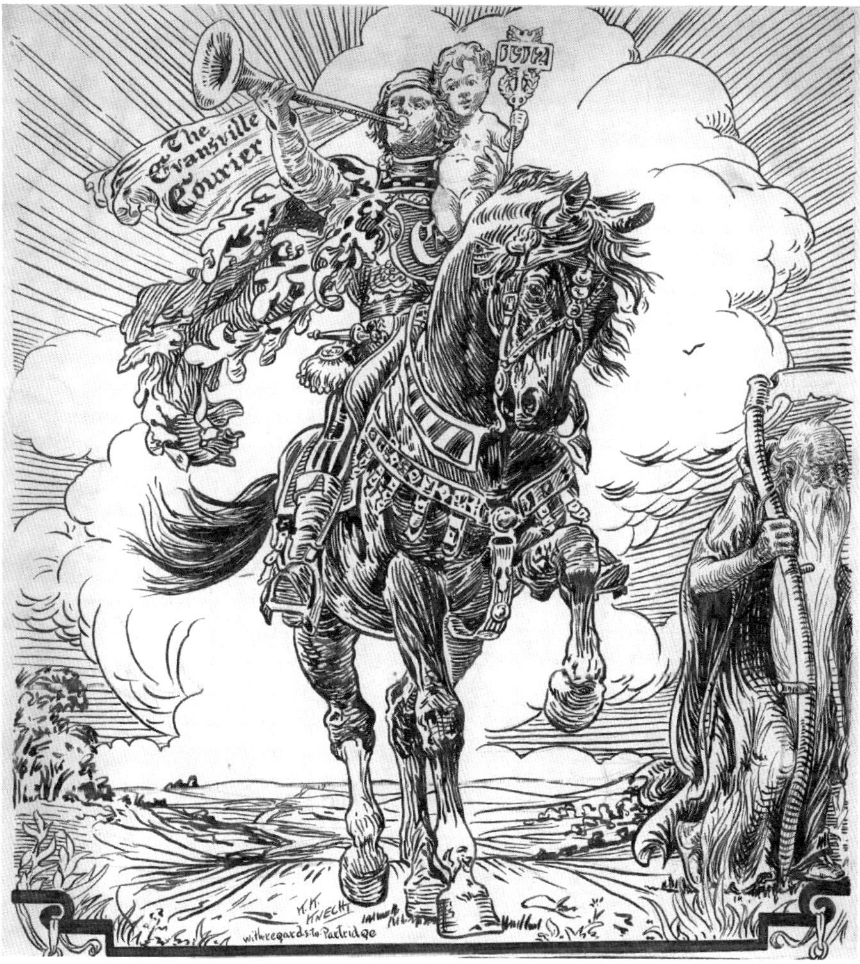

A herald on horseback announcing the New Year, January 1912. *UE/EVPL.*

company, "Herald Announcing the Opening."[147] Knecht's 1912 image is an exact copy—line for line—of that work, with just a couple of minor adjustments; it is so similar that it could only have been done by tracing. Knecht acknowledged that he was in the habit of doing so, writing many years later that in the early period, "I did all the art work, illustrations, sketches and the like [for the *Courier*]. For line drawing from photo [I] used tracing paper over heads or photos…and traced over that on chalk plate for impression. Had no services for those first years, [so I] used much…by clipping half tones from larger city papers etc."[148] While he clearly acknowledges Partridge in the cartoon and was quite open about tracing other images, to a modern sensibility it seems perilously close to the line that divides tribute from plagiarism.

His drawing celebrating the opening of the Henderson-Evansville Ohio River bridge in July 1932 was entitled simply "The Bridge." It is powerful and dramatic, taking a viewpoint from below and to the side of the bridge. It communicates the majesty and impressiveness not just of the bridge but of the river, too. Knecht would have been smiling as he drew this cartoon, as for years he had been an activist in the campaign for the bridge to be built and for it to be built at Evansville. He drew many cartoons that argued eloquently for this cause and that condemned the distractions and special interests that had gotten in its way over the course of the 1920s. These cartoons included an astonishing full-page front-page rendering of an imagined bridge under the headline "A Bridge Across the Ohio Is Evansville's Next Big Job," published on February 6, 1921.

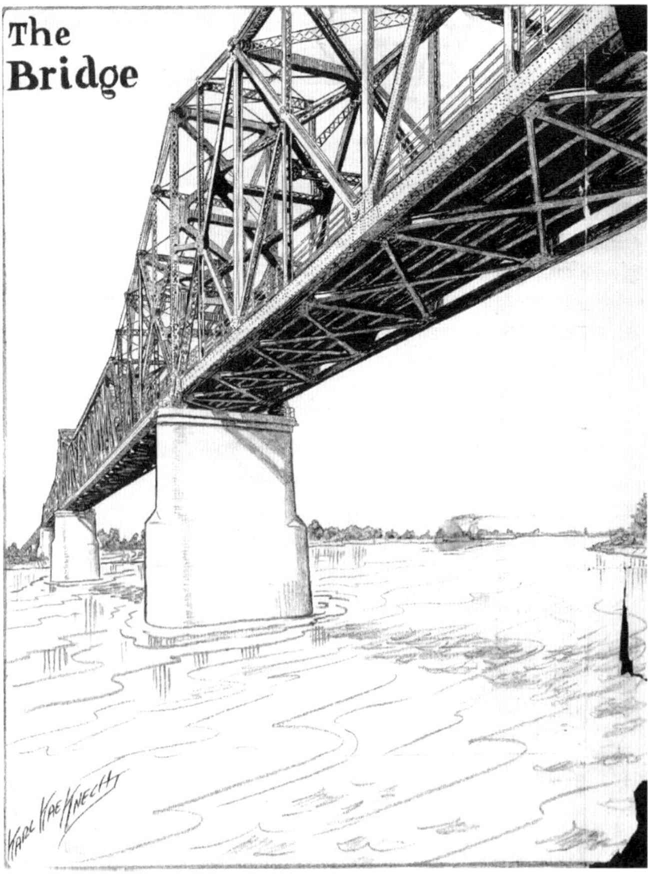

"The Bridge," July 1932. *UE/FVPL.*

Another celebration of a special moment in local history was his 1917 drawing entitled "The Founding of Evansville by Hugh McGary—1817," which was produced for the 1917 special Midsummer Edition of the *Courier*. It must have been a remarkably busy time for Knecht—other large images he drew for that edition included "The Arrival of the First Stage Coach," "Sunset Park Thirty Years Ago," "When Steamboating Was at Its Height on the Ohio," "The Passing Parade" and "Evansville in Civil War Days. Troops Passing at Third and Main Streets, 1861." He also provided three illustrations for a story about Evansville men in the army, as well as the regular front-page cartoon. The McGary drawing is a wonderful imaginative rendering of the mythic moment of the establishment of the city, as founding father Hugh McGary, gun in hand, stares wistfully at the forested riverbanks that one day will become Evansville. He wears a coonskin hat—reminding us perhaps that his father was in fact a "close associate of Daniel Boone"—and there are two Native Americans to his right, rendered with respect and dignity.[149]

The sinking of the *Titanic* on April 15, 1912, was one of the worst disasters of the period, and as a recent writer observed, "It is striking how quickly the *Titanic* became embedded within visual and literary culture

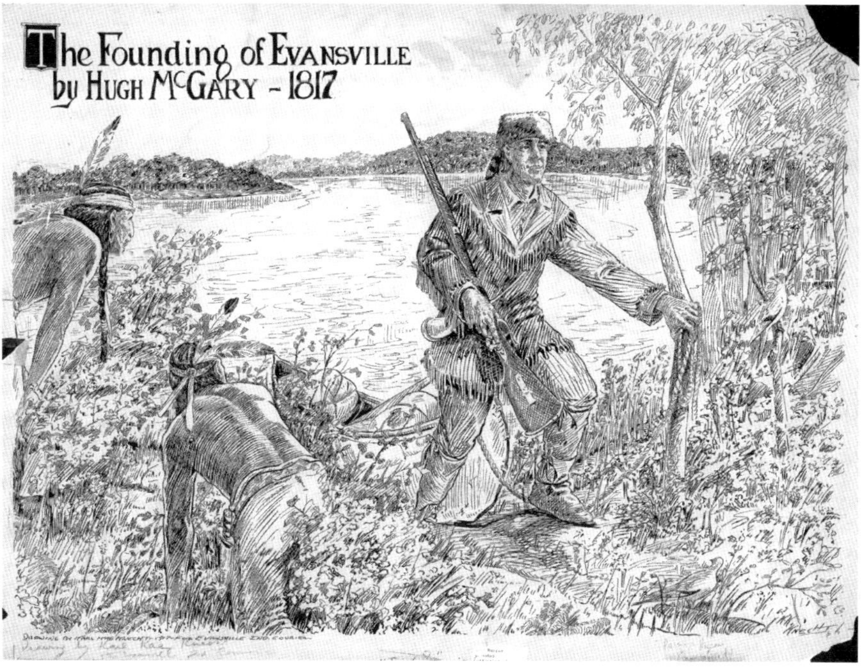

"The Founding of Evansville by Hugh McGary—1917," June 1917. *UE/EVPL.*

from immediately after the disaster in the form of contemporary reportage, photographs of anxious relatives waiting for news at the White Star Line offices, the multitudes of illustrations depicting the ship's collision with the iceberg, publication of the official inquiries and imaginative, filmic and literary meditation on the ship's sinking."[150] It certainly attracted Knecht's attention, and his cartoons on this subject make a remarkable series. His first, published on April 17, 1912, and entitled "Always Lurking Around," depicts an iceberg with a grinning skull of death, lying in wait for the unsuspecting White Star liner and all those on board. One day later, one of his most powerful and poignant cartoons was published. Stark and simple, it shows the *Titanic* passengers' hats and the captain's and crew's caps being tossed in heavy seas; it appeared under the caption "Men Who Were Real Men." On April 19, his cartoon appeared with a double caption—text both above and below the image. It shows surviving women and children disembarking from a rescue vessel at New York Harbor. The top caption is simply "Hoping," and the bottom caption is "That their loved ones might have been picked up by other boats, is the arriving survivor's one comforting thought." His fourth successive *Titanic* cartoon, published on April 20 under the caption "The Way Uncle Sam Would Have Them!," is a savage critique of the steamship companies that he believed would compromise passenger safety in order to offer more luxuries such as tennis courts, swimming pools and theaters but only "a few life boats." Uncle Sam weeps as he looks into the possibility of passenger ships that offered "plenty of life boats to accommodate all on board" as well as "comforts enough to satisfy all." It represents a remarkable pivot from pathos and memorialization to anger and indeed activism.

The final cartoon in Knecht's *Titanic* series, published on April 21, was an extremely powerful one, again making use of the double caption. Entitled "The Tombstones of the Seas," it depicted icebergs as a variety of cemetery monuments, including a cross and an angel. At the center, silhouetted against a jet-black sky, stands a large white obelisk on which is inscribed "To the Titanic Dead. 1912." The caption beneath is "Monuments of Heroes," and beneath that is a remarkable and lengthy statement:

> *Memory of the greatest sea tragedy in history will fade, but icebergs will never look the same. Their appearance will always be a silent reminder of the disaster that befell the world's greatest and largest boat. They will always stand as grim warnings to those who sail the seas to steer clear of such dangers. A costly toll in human lives was exacted, to warn those who ply the seas, that more attention must be paid to safety rather than speed and luxury.*

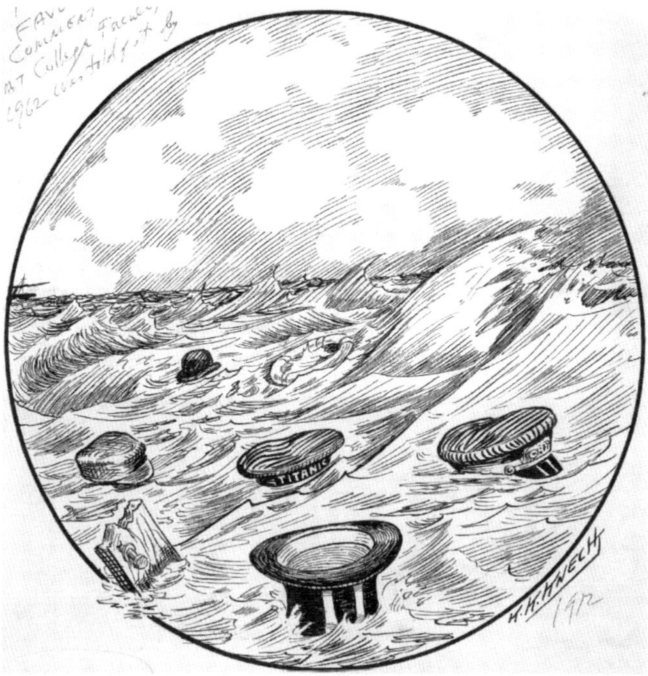

Titanic passengers' hats and the captain's and crew's caps, April 18, 1912. *UE/EVPL.*

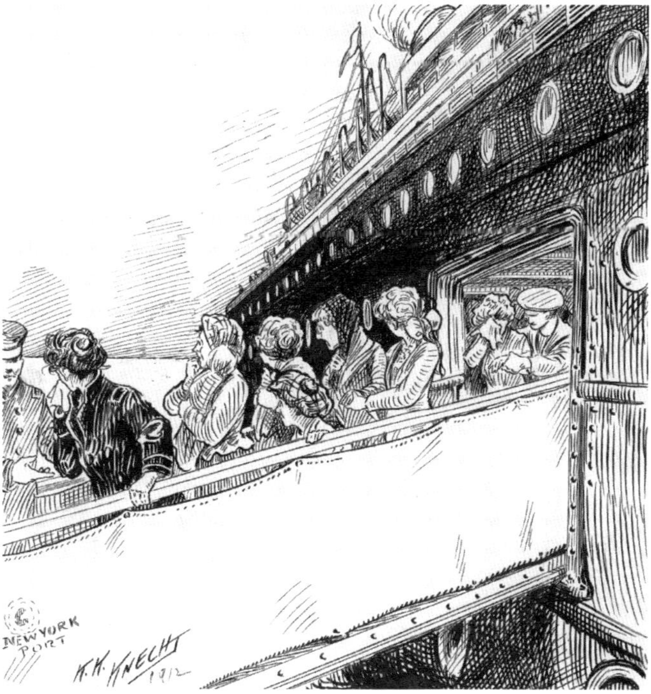

Titanic survivors arriving at port, April 19, 1912. *UE/EVPL.*

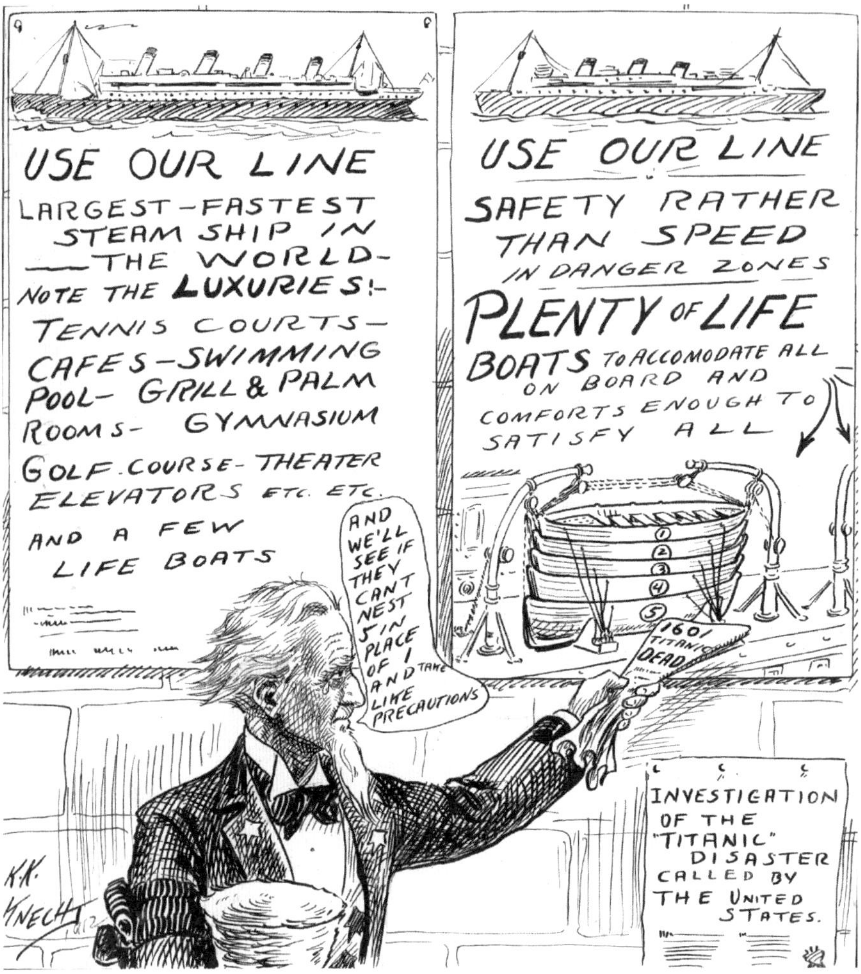

Titanic and Uncle Sam, April 20, 1912. *UE/EVPL.*

Once again Karl Kae Knecht is providing a complex and multilayered message that is poignant and respectful of the dead while at the same time being critical and activist.

His view that such disasters were a product of lax enforcement was also seen very obviously four years later in cartoons that responded to the terrible loss of the Chicago passenger excursion ship the SS *Eastland*, which rolled over at its dock on the Chicago River on July 25, 1915, killing over eight hundred people. Among the dead were twenty-two complete families.[151] Knecht's first cartoon was in itself a powerful and striking image—depicting the ship being rolled over by the giant bony finger of Death.[152] A tragedy has taken place, but he places no blame. It could even be interpreted as a capricious act by the fickle finger of fate. But the next day, Knecht links this disaster to four others: a figure of Father Time tells a figure marked "Safety First" about a series of "Past Disasters." On the list are the Iroquois theater fire of 1903, which killed over six hundred people; the 1904 *Slocum* excursion boat fire, in which over one thousand people died; the sinking of the *Titanic* in 1912; and the 1914 sinking of the RMS *Empress of Ireland*, in which over one thousand people died.[153] Although the figure receiving "another lesson" in this cartoon is sweating and weeping, the message is rather ambiguous and again assigns no blame. His July 27 cartoon, however, is very different. It is captioned "How About It?," and it is an emphatic and powerful image of a courtroom scene. A large hand belonging to the "Public" points an accusatory or even judging finger at "Officialdom," a hat-wringing figure in the dock, while Public's other hand slams down a piece of paper inscribed "Prospects of future disasters, wholly man-made, wholly avoidable, wholly inexcusable." The Iroquois, the *Slocum* and the *Eastland* disasters are all described as "man-made disasters" and "wholly avoidable." Knecht has finally got around to apportioning blame, and in this environment, his chosen target is officials whose negligent enforcement of rules and codes were believed to have contributed to all of these disasters.

It is clear that this was part of a wider agenda promoted by Knecht, part of the Progressive era commitment to activism on behalf of the safety of regular working people in America, a product of what the U.S. Department of Labor has called the "great interest during the Progressive Era in investigation and amelioration of hazardous working conditions."[154] It was certainly needed; as David Von Drehle said, "Death was an almost routine workplace hazard in those days."[155] After the 1911 Triangle Shirtwaist Factory Fire in New York City that claimed the lives of 146 workers, Knecht drew a cartoon that unflinchingly showed the disaster unfolding. He depicted desperate workers calling for help from windows while flames surge all around them; another worker dangles from a ledge. The cartoon was captioned "When Building Ordinances Are Not Enforced" and gloomily predicted that "Calamities like that…will go on."[156] And as has been seen with his response to the *Titanic* disaster, Knecht was willing to go beyond mere criticism of enforcement and, for example, offer a critique of the shipping companies whom he saw as being responsible for maritime disasters. That is seen to an even more remarkable degree in his response to the sinking of the SS *Vestris* in 1928, in which over one hundred people died.

His forceful and unambiguous cartoon of November 16, 1928, spoke of "unsafe life boats, improper equipment in life boats, [and] improper handling when launched," as well as "a crew that would delay in sending S.O.S., delay lowering life boats [and] delay warning passengers." Most striking of all, the cartoon depicts an inspector asleep at his desk and an owner who is only concerned that "we ought to make good money on this trip."[157]

Obviously, the biggest single event of this time period was World War I, something that killed around ten million people and injured millions more while arguably doing more to shape the modern world than anything else. Knecht drew many cartoons that focused on the war, including a noteworthy effort on August 5, 1914, the day after Britain declared war on Germany, that showed the German kaiser as a circus animal trainer being confronted by the Russian bear and the lion of Britain (Knecht says "England") under the caption "Now He Has Got His Hands Full!" The United States, of course, did not join the war until 1917, and the image of the American doughboy from 1917 is a celebration of that. A smiling young man labeled "Evansville" strides boldly forward, with his rifle on his right shoulder while he waves his army hat in the air with his left hand. In the background hang three sets of U.S. Army uniforms, from the Mexican-American War of 1846, the Civil War and the Spanish-American War of 1898. The theme of continuity of military service and the connectedness of one generation of American soldiers to another was one he would return to on several other occasions, most notably during World War II when he more than once depicted old soldiers from nineteenth century wars as brothers of the young men currently serving.[158]

World War I had a strong Evansville connection—hundreds of local men served, and eighty-five died in uniform, many of them killed in action and most of the rest killed by the influenza epidemic, the so-called Spanish flu, that raged around the world between 1918 and 1920.[159] November 3, 1917, saw the first three American servicemen to be killed in action in France. One of them was James Bethel Gresham, who was born in Kentucky but raised and educated in Evansville. His body was eventually returned, and he is buried in the city's Locust Hill Cemetery. Knecht drew a beautiful portrait of Gresham on his death in 1917—another reminder of Knecht's ability as an artist. On November 11, his cartoon showed Gresham's mother, Alice Dodd, on whom much of the city's memorializing energy was focused. She is dressed in black, sitting on a flag-draped chair in front of a full-length portrait of her son. She holds a laurel wreath and on either side of her stand figures representing Evansville and Uncle Sam, heads bowed in respect.

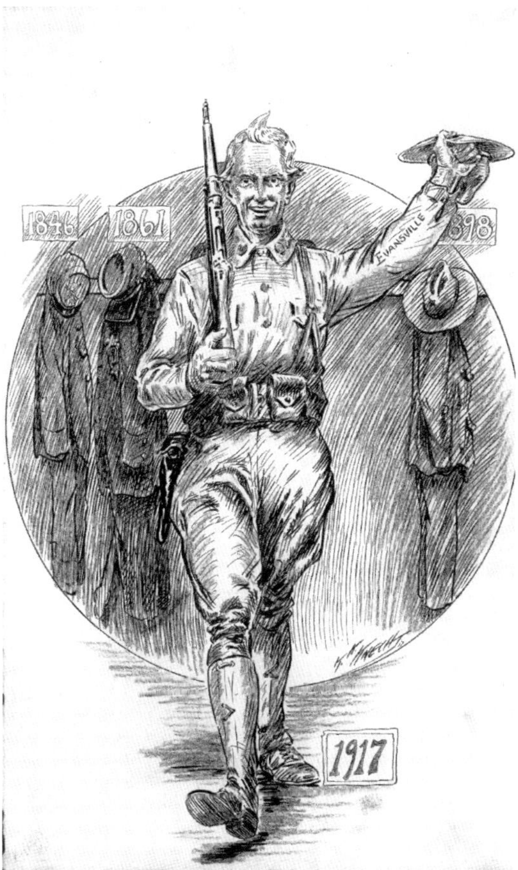

Evansville doughboy, 1917. *UE/EVPL.*

The cartoon advertises the upcoming memorial services to Gresham in the Evansville Coliseum, and the figure of Evansville holds a scroll inscribed "*The Evansville Courier* Fund by popular subscription to build a home for the mother of hero James Bethel Gresham to be a memorial home." On the day after, November 12, 1917, he drew an arresting front-page cartoon captioned "She Gave Her Son—What Are You Giving?" On the left side, it featured a young man pointing out at the viewer, reminiscent of the iconic Uncle Sam recruiting poster by James Montgomery Flagg, produced originally one year earlier—"you could go to the right or the left of that picture and Uncle Sam's eyes still seemed fastened on you with that commanding glare."[160] He is holding a sign that says "*Courier*'s James Gresham Hero Home Fund. A home for his Mother—the first US mother to lose a son in the war with Germany—a memorial for Evansville and her soldier son." The right side of the cartoon is a portrait of Gresham's mother.

As so often, Knecht was being an artistic activist for a civic cause. The previous day Mayor Bosse had introduced her to a crowd of five thousand at the Coliseum who "gave a rousing ovation that swelled to the roof, but still retained the solemnity of tribute to the fallen hero and his mother."[161] The campaign led by Knecht and the *Courier* was ultimately successful, and less than one year later, the city presented to Mrs. Dodd a home located in Garvin Park.[162] On November 19, 1917, Knecht drew a cartoon that

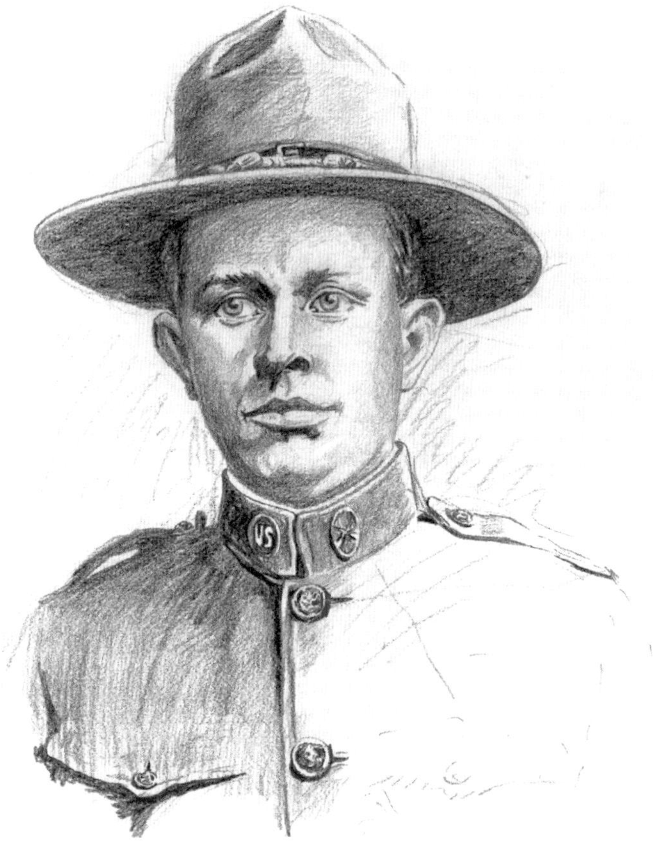

James Bethel Gresham, November 1917. *UE/EVPL.*

showed the erection of a monument, presumably by the American people, as Uncle Sam's coat and hat are hanging up nearby. The monument is marked "For World Democracy," and the very first stone—the foundation, or base, of the monument—is inscribed "James B. Gresham, Evansville, Ind." The poignant caption is simply "At the Base." What is remarkable about this image is that Knecht reused it two decades later when he included it in another cartoon that was yet again part of a civic campaign, this time by the Indiana Veterans of Foreign Wars to raise money for a Gresham memorial at Dress Plaza at the city's riverfront.[163] The original cartoon is pasted in at top right while at lower right is a line drawing of the "Monument built by the French at Bathelmont France near [the] place where Gresham, first American soldier, was killed in [the] World War." The left-hand side shows schoolchildren depositing coins into a collection jar while Kay salutes with a bayonetted rifle. When Gresham's body came home to Evansville in 1921, Knecht drew a cartoon on July 15 that was an extremely powerful antiwar statement: an enormous figure of a bareheaded Uncle Sam holding the flag-draped coffin, saying, "And I trust that this first shall be the last of firsts." All of these cartoons together communicate rather well not just the importance of James Bethel Gresham to Evansville but also his importance to Karl Kae Knecht.

The next two cartoons to be studied in this section deal with the city of Evansville's most fundamental physical feature, one that has had huge ramifications both positive and negative—its location on the Ohio River. His magnificent 1926 cartoon entitled "Our Giant" personifies the river as a mighty beast of burden. Not just any mighty beast of course—this is, after all, Karl Kae Knecht—the Ohio River is here depicted as an enormous elephant, many times bigger than life size. The drawing communicates the immense power of the river and also its immense potential, assuming it could be controlled and navigated and exploited through dams, bridges and an "Evansville River Terminal." Knecht was a consistent advocate for all three of these, as he was for all kinds of infrastructure projects that would benefit his adopted city. As seen already, the Evansville Henderson Bridge

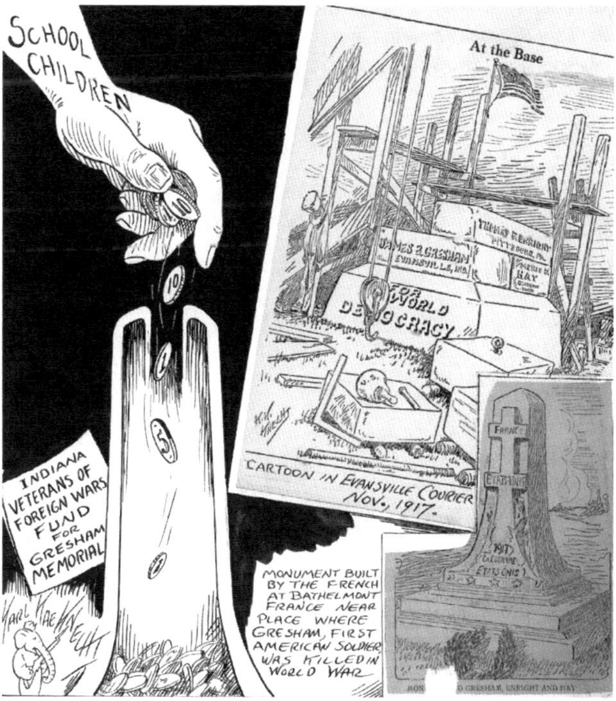

Gresham Memorial Fund, 1936. *UE/EVPL.*

was to come in 1932, and the Mead Johnson river terminal was opened in February 1931.[164] The river dwarfs the men in the picture, but the men are still in control—barely—as shown by the figure in the foreground who is guiding the beast with an elephant hook.

But man was not really in control, as seen in the greatest disaster in Evansville history, the flood of 1937, which is the subject of the next cartoon, captioned "As the Wild Waves Leave." The flood was a massive disaster across much of the Midwest—David Welky called it "the worst river flood in American history." In the words of James E. Castro: "'Hell and High Water' was the way *Time* magazine of February 1, 1937, described the flood, and the description could not have been more accurate. The raging floodwaters inundated thousands of homes and businesses, factories and farms in a half dozen states, drove a million people from their homes, claimed nearly

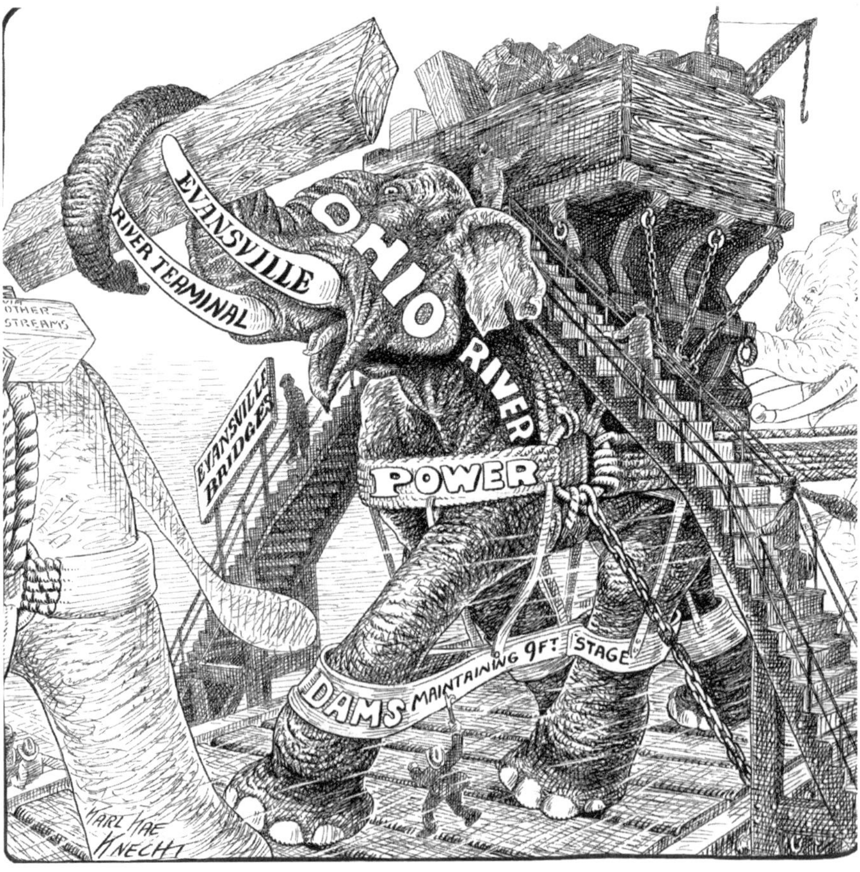

Ohio River as a mighty elephant, 1926. *UE/EVPL.*

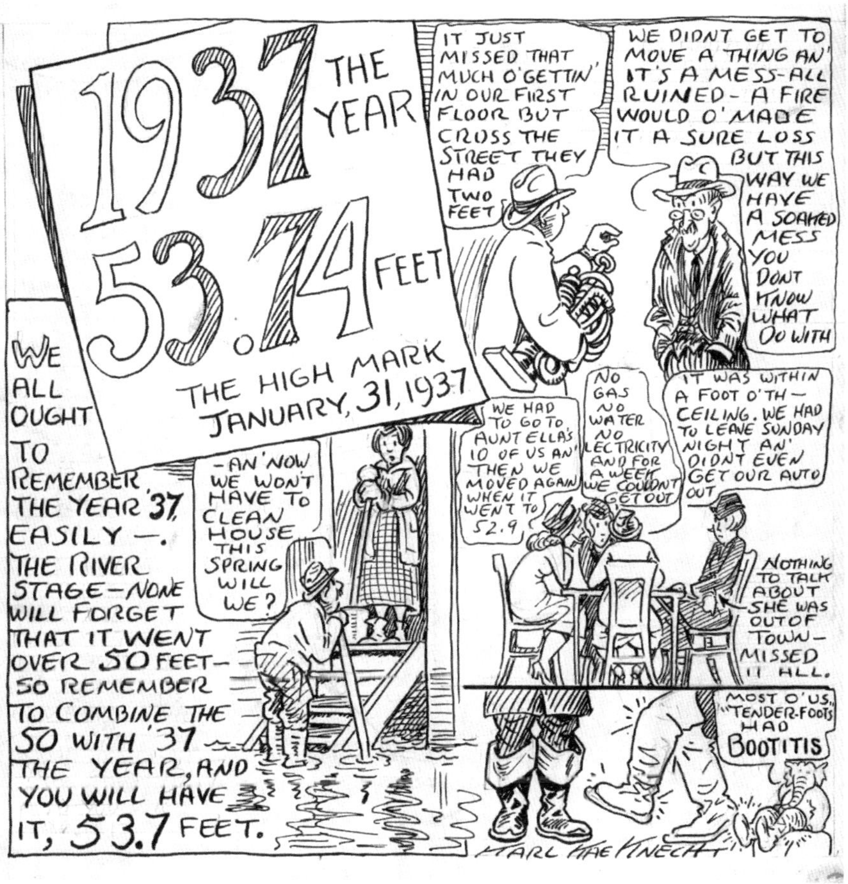

"As the Wild Waves Leave," 1937. *UE/EVPL.*

400 lives, and recorded $500 million in damages."[165] Evansville was hit extremely hard; experienced local journalist Rich Davis said in 2007 that it was "the greatest natural disaster in the history of Evansville." Over seven thousand homes were affected as the Ohio River rose nineteen feet above its flood stage.[166] Five hundred city blocks were flooded, and "many of the old commercial buildings along the waterfront on Riverside Avenue and First Street were so battered and weakened by the waves that they either collapsed or had to be torn down."

The cost to the city was astronomical, and the iconic photographs of the devastation—many of them taken by Knecht himself—almost defy belief today.[167] Knecht's cartoon is a brilliant example of another aspect of his style—this drawing is gently pedagogic, providing a wealth of information in a warm and amusing manner. The key fact—that the river crested at 53.74 feet on January 31, 1937—is communicated powerfully, and then a series of amusing little vignettes tell other parts of the story. In the corner, Kay complains about her sore feet from having to wear wading boots for so long. It is also a reminder that sometimes the cartoonist's role is to provide comfort—this is an image that would have allowed an exhausted and shaken community to pause for a moment and smile, perhaps even laugh. And then, led by Mr. Public and his impressive biceps, they could get back to the hard work of cleaning up.

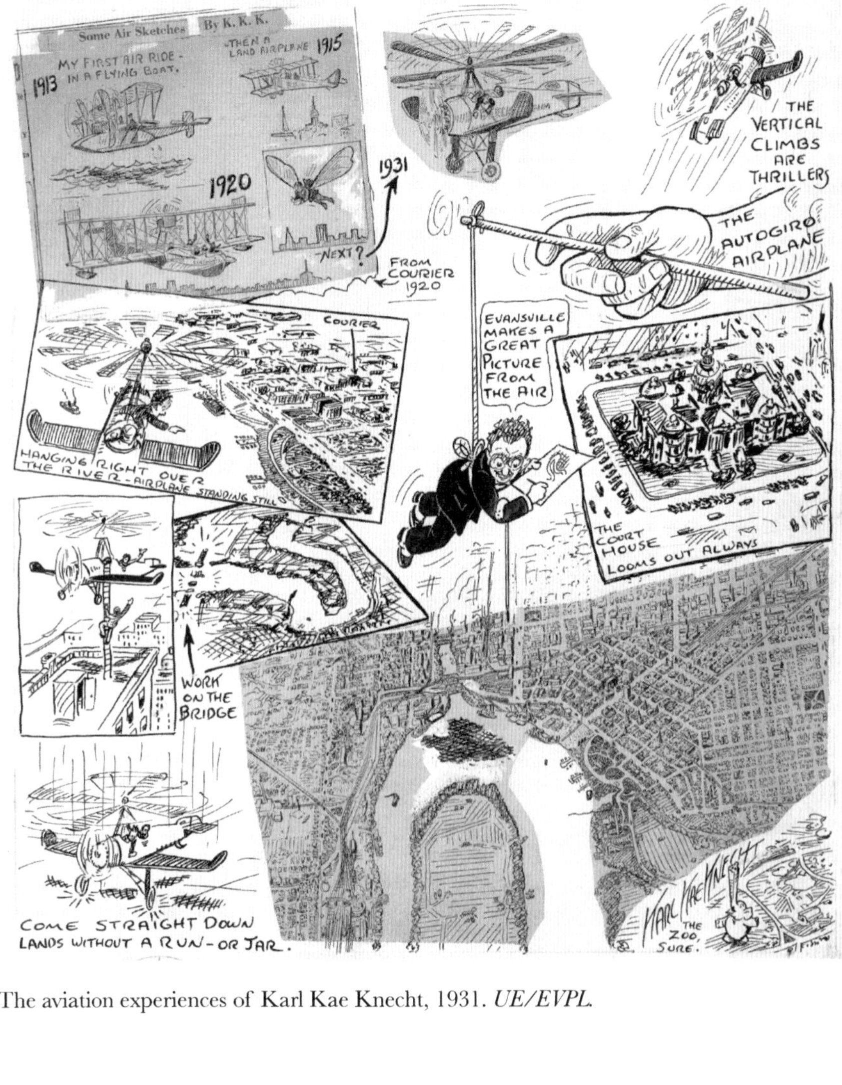

The aviation experiences of Karl Kae Knecht, 1931. *UE/EVPL.*

As has been seen already, Knecht was an aviation enthusiast, going on early flights, taking aerial photographs, drawing many aerial views of the city and advocating for an Evansville airport and its subsequent growth over the years. His 1931 cartoon of his own aviation experiences is a wonderful little showcase of his talents and quirks. He often drew self-portraits, and in this one, he places himself right in the middle of a series of drawings that are aerial views of Evansville. As he often did, he includes a pair of previous drawings and cleverly interweaves them with the new; in this case, the "new" is literally the newest type of airplane in existence—what Knecht calls the "autogiro airplane," which made its Evansville debut in September 1931, wowing a crowd of thousands at the airport.[168] Among the landmarks that he picks out for special mention are the zoo, the courthouse, the Ohio River bridge and his own place of work, the downtown offices of the *Courier*.

And the *Courier* is the subject of the next cartoon, a historical work from 1921 that discusses the development of printing presses, starting with a ghostly Gutenberg-era press at top left. A nineteenth-century press from the time "when the *Courier* was still young" dominates the top panel—presumably from around the middle of the century, as the paper was founded in 1845. In 1910, the paper described its earliest manifestation like this: "In 1845 *The Courier* was a four-page, five-column newspaper, dingy in appearance and poor in news. At the time, however, it ranked with all other newspapers throughout the central west and surpassed many of them."[169] By 1921, new technology was changing the printing industry and the *Evansville Press* was boasting of its new fifty-four-ton Goss printing machine, a "New High Speed Printing Machine of the Latest Pattern" with thirty-six thousand separate parts.[170] Perhaps this is what forced Knecht to produce this drawing—the bottom part of which he had drawn for a completely different cartoon in 1915. It is a rather astonishing piece of recycling. The words "our new press" from 1915 were erased and the date "1921" was added to the drawing. The speech balloon on the left is actually partially the same as six years earlier, with some words whited out and replaced. Despite that, the whole works together very well, the drawings are intricate and attractive and it is an interesting example of Knecht's willingness to repurpose old images for new circumstances.

No discussion of American life in the 1920s and 1930s would be complete without considering two of the biggest phenomena of the era and, indeed, of all American history: Prohibition and the Great Depression. Karl Kae Knecht of course drew many cartoons that considered these two experiences, and this chapter will close by studying two cartoons on each topic.

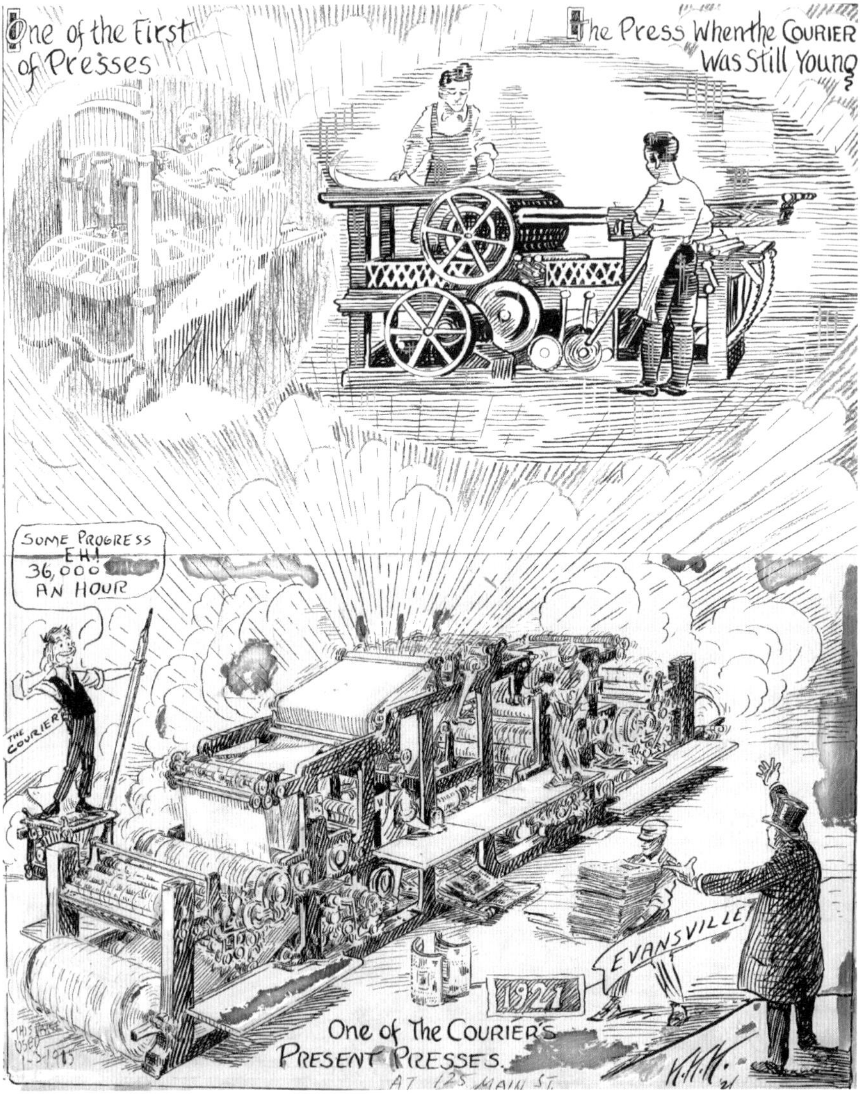

The history of printing presses, 1921. *UE/EVPL.*

Prohibition refers to the thirteen-year period between 1920 and 1933 when, under the Eighteenth Amendment, "the manufacture, sale, or transportation of intoxicating liquors" was prohibited.[171] Its effects were, of course, to drive these activities underground and create a gigantic black market and a vast network of smuggling that made massive fortunes for many people and led to the violent death of countless others. "For all its outrageously intolerant overtones, its hypocrisy and double standards," said

Edward Behr, "Prohibition represented a genuine attempt to better the lives of people. That it did them instead untold harm—that America has never fully recovered from the legacy of these thirteen years—should come as no surprise. As history keeps telling us—but do we ever listen?—the road to hell is paved with good intentions."[172]

Knecht's cartoon from 1929 is a very amusing depiction of alcohol smuggling in Florida around the infamous Belle Isle. (He spells it incorrectly.) The island held the mansion of the department store magnate J.C. Penney, at which President Herbert Hoover vacationed in early 1929. Hoover is shown out on a fishing trip, catching a crate of illicit booze. It was also close

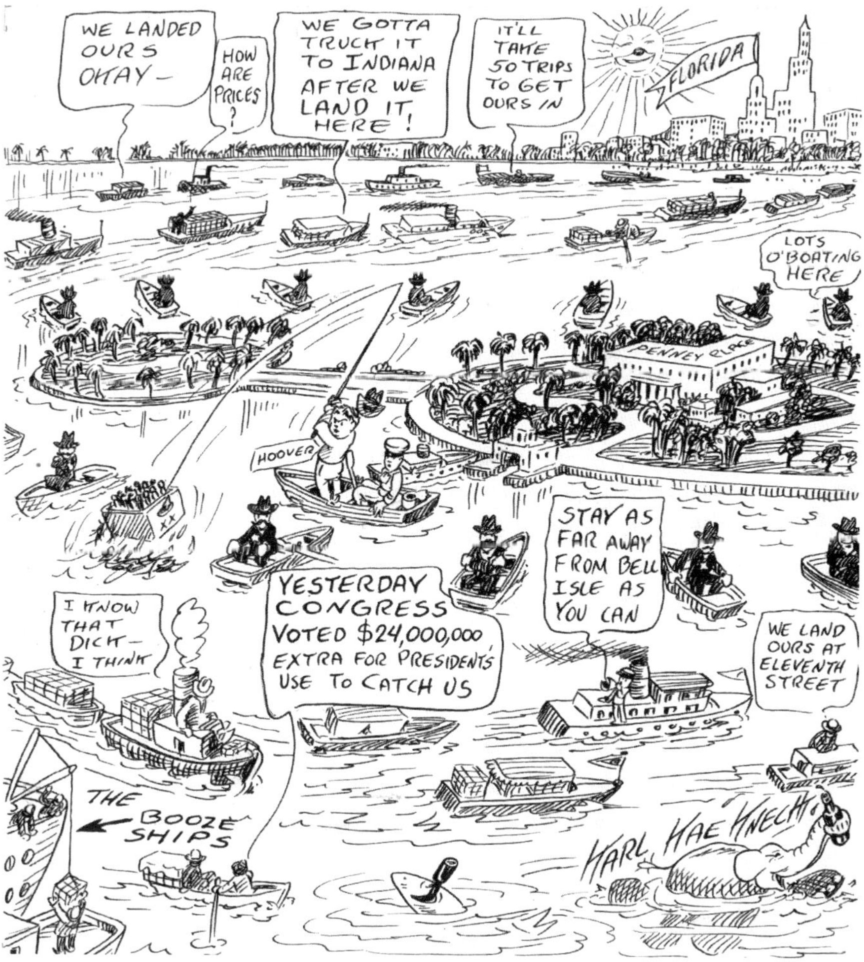

Prohibition smuggling boats in Florida, 1929. *UE/EVPL.*

to mobster Al Capone's villa on Palm Island, which might help explain its central role in illicit alcohol transportation.[173] In this picture, the island is surrounded by grim-faced law enforcement, and one smuggler warns the other to "stay as far away from Bell[e] Isle as you can." In the bottom right, Kay, too, gets involved, swimming along with an open bottle of alcohol in her trunk.

The second Knecht cartoon dealing with Prohibition is a retrospective assessment, drawn on the death of its architect, Andrew J. Volstead, and published on January 24, 1947. His was the act of Congress that formally carried out the purpose of the Eighteenth Amendment and "set the rules for National Prohibition,"[174] and Knecht calls him the "father of the Volstead Prohibition Act that made the 18th Amendment." What is truly conspicuous about this cartoon is how unequivocally Knecht condemns the whole Prohibition enterprise. A smirking Al Capone features with equal prominence to Volstead himself, symbolizing the fact that organized crime was the era's biggest beneficiary, and when Knecht lists the outcomes of Prohibition, they are all negative. "Criminal organizations," "rackets," "gang wars" and "bootlegging" all flow from the "Prohibition Era," which is itself symbolized by a sealed and padlocked bottle.

Before Prohibition was even over, the Wall Street crash took place, and the Great Depression began. Knecht's June 1933 cartoon of a figure representing the Depression being strangled by the ubiquitous symbol of the National Recovery Administration (NRA), the Blue Eagle, is dramatic and powerful. The NRA was one of the central policies of Roosevelt's first hundred days in office and one of the central planks of what has been called the First New Deal. Tim McNeese said recently:

> *The NRA's overarching purpose was to solve the problems of economic instability, overproduction, and labor-management issues by carrying out economic planning. Representing industrial leaders, labor leaders, and government bureaucrats, the NRA created new "codes" of competition. The codes were based on limiting production while setting prices and workers' hours and wages....The strict rules of capitalism took a back seat to the latent socialism of the NRA.*[175]

This is an optimistic cartoon. Kay tells the figure representing the Depression, "You'd better wave the white flag," and it certainly seems like the Blue Eagle very much has the upper hand. While this optimism was misplaced—the U.S. Supreme Court declared the NRA unconstitutional

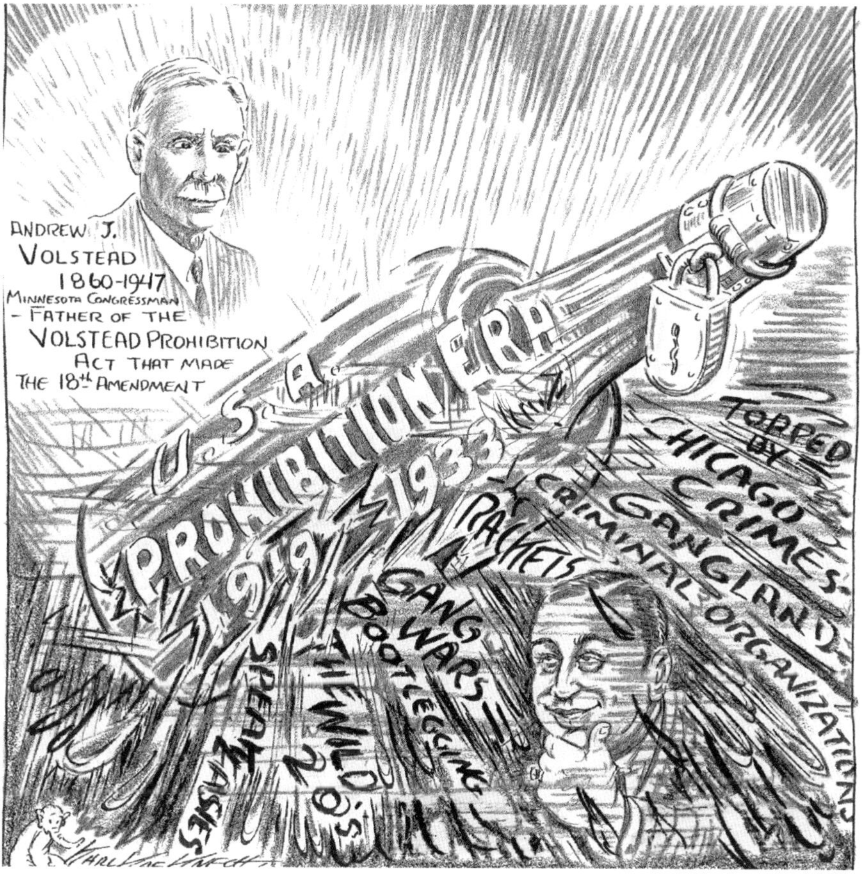

Volstead, architect of Prohibition, January 24, 1947. *UE/EVPL.*

in 1935, and in many ways, the Depression did not end until the gigantic stimulus of World War II—it was by no means unique to Knecht in 1933. The historian Robert S. McElvaine wrote:

> *The largest parade in the history of New York City saw 250,000 people march down Fifth Avenue for the Blue Eagle….For a brief time in the summer of 1933 it was believable that the country was marching back to prosperity. During the months between Roosevelt's inauguration and the effective dates of the NRA codes in the fall, production and employment increased significantly. The index of factory production, which had hit a low of 56 in March, rose to 101 in July 1933.*[176]

People were excited—the possibility of the Depression being quickly defeated seemed real. And Knecht's cartoon both reflected and perpetuated that view.

The role of the Supreme Court in ending the NRA was vital, and of course, the court was a key player in the whole period of the Depression and the New Deal. The second cartoon of this period, from February 12, 1937, deals with another massively contentious Supreme Court story—FDR's so-called court-packing plan of that year. It brilliantly ties together one of the biggest national stories of 1937 with Evansville's own biggest story of the year, the great flood. Dismayed by the Supreme Court's consistent rulings against New Deal policies over the course of the decade, most notably on "Black Monday," May 27, 1935, when three unanimous court decisions killed vital New Deal measures, FDR planned to add justices who would be

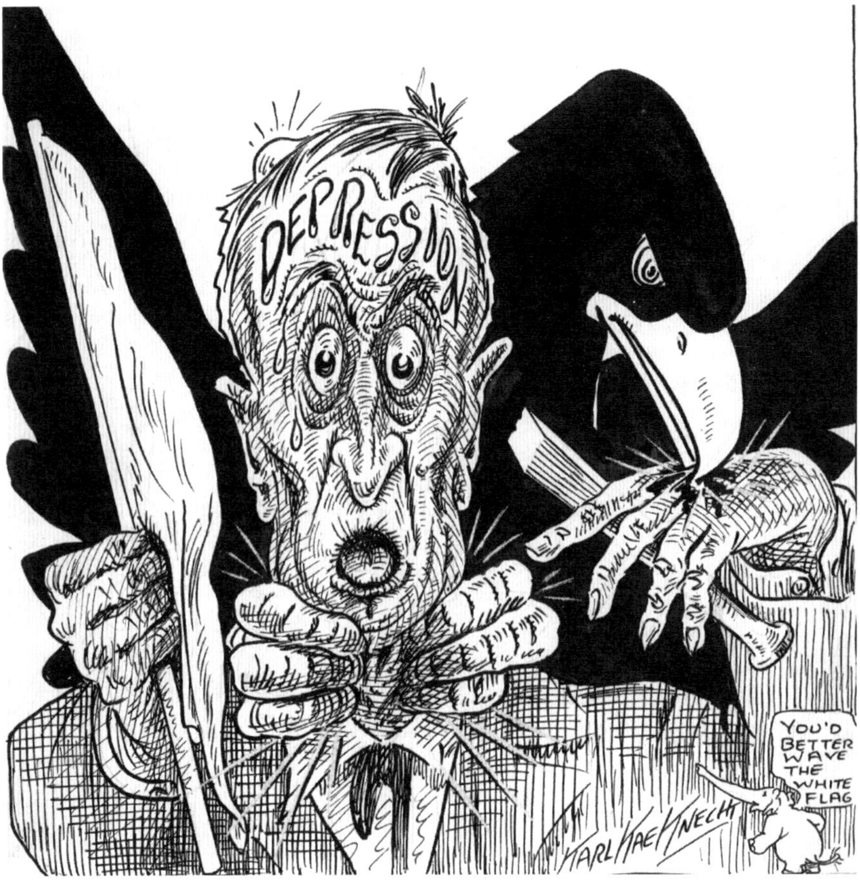

Depression strangled by the NRA, June 1933. *UE/EVPL.*

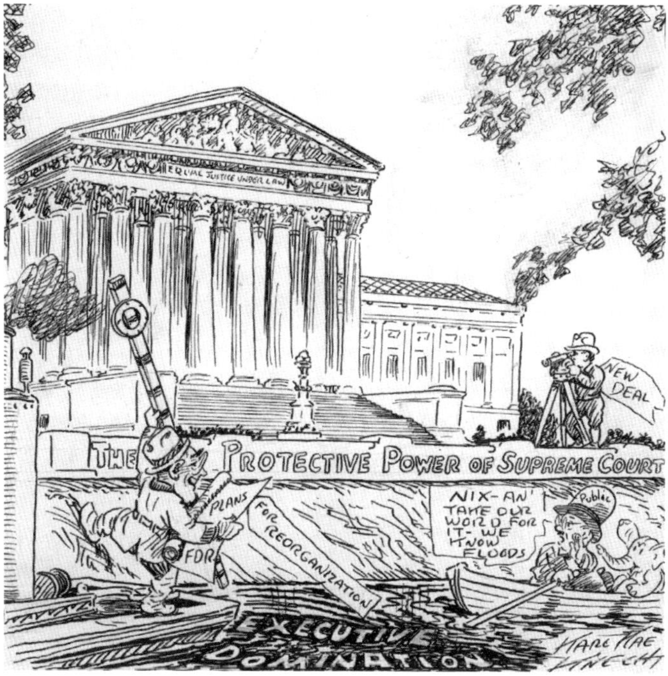

FDR's attempted court packing, February 12, 1937. *UE/EVPL.*

supportive of his policies. This was done with the Judicial Procedures Reform Bill of 1937, the subject of this cartoon.[177] It is a strong and unequivocal condemnation of what was seen by many members of the public to be an action that would have disrupted the delicate separation of powers in U.S. politics; "the Protective Power of the Supreme Court" is here threatened by the rising floodwaters of "Executive Domination." While FDR seems delighted at the situation, Mr. Public and Kay express their firm disapproval, based on bitter experience: "Take our word for it—we know floods." In many respects, Mr. Public here is speaking for a broad consensus, as in the end, the plan failed because of, among other things, "adverse public opinion."[178] Again, Knecht produces a cartoon that reflected and perhaps helped shape local public opinion.

The years 1903 to 1939 were a period of dramatic and tumultuous change in the United States and the wider world, and it is reasonable to say the same about Karl Kae Knecht. In these years, he developed from an untested neophyte being given a chance on a small provincial daily to a seasoned and venerated editorial cartoonist on a prominent regional newspaper and a man whose activism profoundly affected the community in which he lived. He had done great things, but his golden age lay ahead; it was to come with World War II.

Chapter 5

CARTOONS 1939–45

World War II was arguably "the most destructive event in recorded human history"[179] and one of the most pivotal watershed moments that has ever taken place; it was also probably the most important period of Karl Kae Knecht's professional life. The world of the past seventy-five years is in many respects the creation of that war. Knecht certainly grasped the enormity of the conflict, and during the war years, almost every single day saw him produce cartoons that were centered on the war.[180] This section will consider first the cartoons that reflected the wider, international scope of the war and will then move on to discuss the cartoons that dealt with the homefront.

The first cartoon in this section was published on August 28, 1939, under the caption "Will It, Eventually, Be Just a Bear Hug or a Bear Squeeze?" It is one of the most prophetic cartoons that Knecht ever drew, getting as it did to the incongruity of the marriage of convenience that was the German-Soviet Nonaggression Pact (the Molotov–Ribbentrop Pact) of August 1939, something that "fascinated and puzzled cartoonists" around the world.[181] As Knecht observed in this drawing, while both sides were smiling and hugging, their fundamental mutual incompatibility was just under the surface, here symbolized by the discarded scourge and sickle at their feet. In the end, of course, it would be Hitler's decision to break the pact and invade the USSR in the summer of 1941 that would turn out to be the single most momentous decision of the war and perhaps of the twentieth century.[182] And in the end, the "Bear Squeeze" was to destroy Nazi Germany—a very significant percentage of all German military deaths during World War II happened on the eastern front.[183]

As was seen earlier in this book, Knecht tended to be optimistic and positive, but there were also some cartoons that vigorously communicated the seriousness of the situation. This was especially true in 1942, when the Allies were staring into the abyss; Germany was running wild across Europe and the USSR, and the Japanese were having everything go their way in the Pacific. In a cartoon of February 11, 1942, entitled "When Will You Realize?," Knecht shows a terrified Mr. Public being held by his hand while he teeters on the edge of a crumbling bridge. The bridge is supported by a variety of pillars that represent locations in the Pacific and across the world. The pillars that have snapped thus far, symbolizing falling to the Japanese, are the Pacific Islands, Singapore and the Philippines. Those that are still standing—some of which are cracking—include Burma, Java, Pearl Harbor (patched up), the Panama Canal and ultimately Alaska. Kay also looks terrified. The key to this brilliant cartoon is the presence of Uncle Sam's feet, standing firm at top right while his strong hand supports Public; the implication is that American firmness, calmness and strength will save the

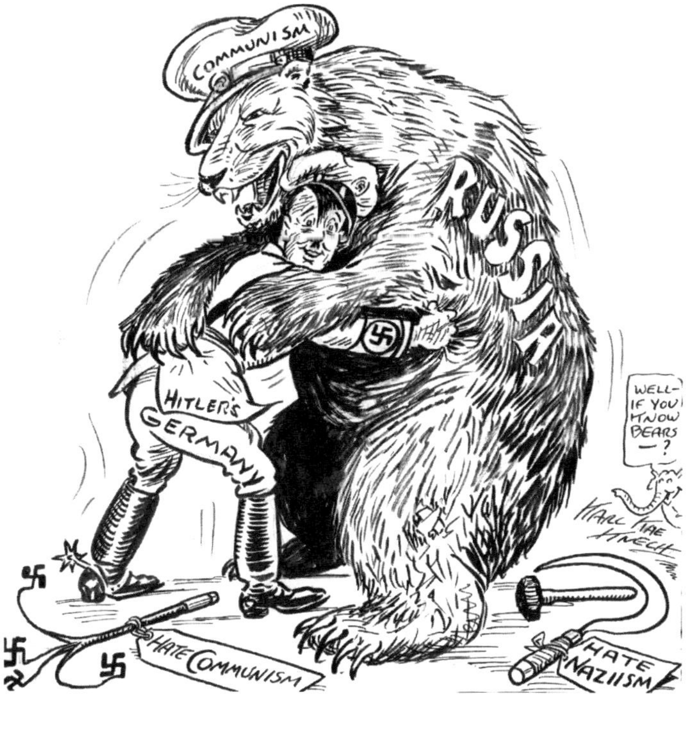

"Will It, Eventually, Be Just a Bear Hug or a Bear Squeeze?" August 28, 1939. *UE/EVPL.*

day. But the risks are stark. The bridge *could* collapse. This was a war that could be lost.

Another spectacular cartoon that spelled out the stakes was drawn in October 9, 1943, and appeared under the caption "A Brute That Is More Terrible Than Any Wild One." Civilians at a circus look at a caged gorilla who says that he is insulted by the image on the right, which is a wild savage gorilla representing Nazi Germany. This gorilla holds a bloody cudgel while destroying a series of classical structures, including a church; a dead child lies on the ground. In his right arm is a bloodied female victim with torn clothes, representing a brutalized and possibly raped "civilization." The image is a fascinating one partly because, as will be seen, he used an almost identical image during the Cold War and partly because he simultaneously uses the trope of the gorilla-as-savage-beast while also communicating his belief in the gentle intelligence of these animals. The talking gorilla in the circus belies the savage beast of propaganda, but at the same time, the savage beast is certainly there to scare his audience. It is a familiar image—one of America's best-known propaganda posters from World War I was "Destroy This Mad Brute" by H.R. Hopps, which depicted basically the same scene:

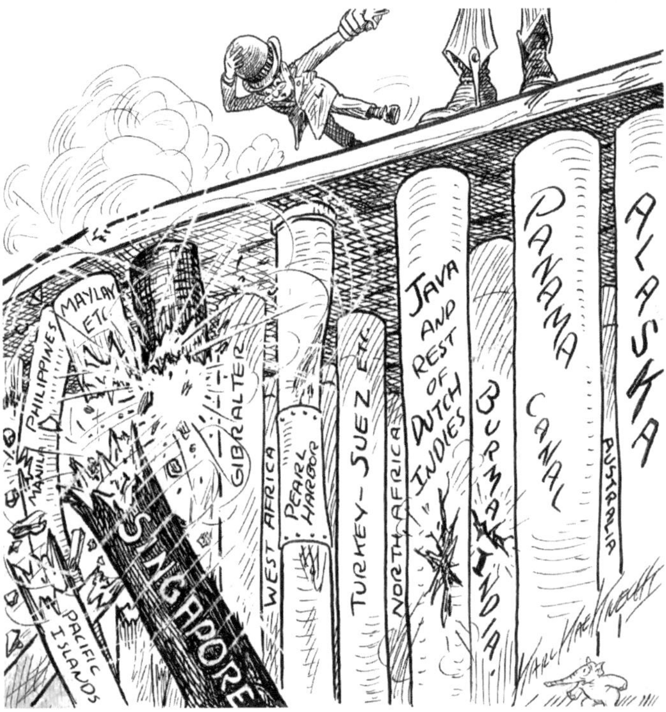

"When Will You Realize?" February 11, 1942. *UE/EVPL*.

"The primitive Hun…morphed into a savage gorilla in this highly sexualized rendition of German militarism."[184] Knecht here is taking advantage of the public perception of gorillas. As Constance Clark has argued, "These gentle animals often carried sensational, even salacious metaphorical freight—and racial connotations—in European and American popular culture.…Gorillas in particular carried associations with rapacious sexuality and with race, through, for example, the freighted term 'miscegenation.'"[185] While there are two gorillas in this drawing, one of them is plainly more significant than the other; Knecht leaves his audience in no doubt as to what is at stake here—this war, he says, is a battle for civilization itself.

The reality of war is further laid bare in a March 20, 1942 cartoon, one of Knecht's starkest, captioned "While They Go Through All Hell's

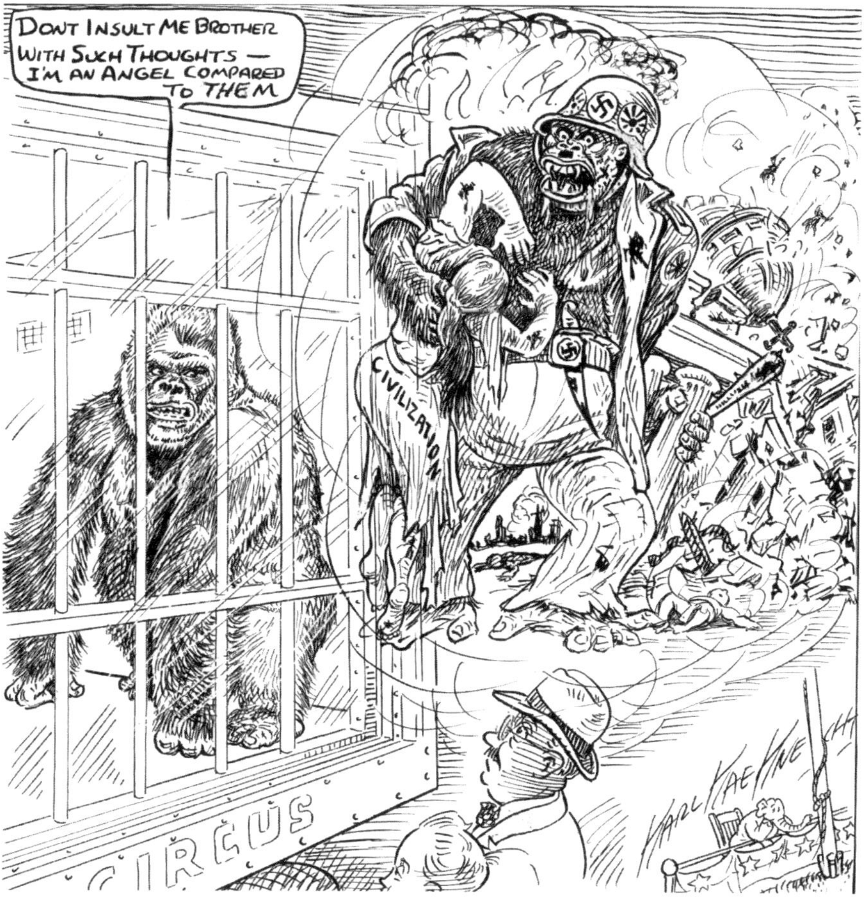

Nazism is depicted as a gorilla, October 9, 1943. *UE/EVPL.*

Fire—and More." It contrasts the petty demands of both management and labor at home with the sacrifices of the men at the front, and it offers an explicit depiction of the experience of war at land, sea and air. Heavy artillery fires, planes crash and burn, ships are sinking, men engage in fierce hand-to-hand combat and, most stunning of all, soldiers die. At bottom right, at least two American soldiers are dead; the fingers of one actually cross the border of the drawing. This is a full year and a half before any American outlet published a single photo of American war dead; in September 1943, *Life* printed the now iconic photo of "Three Dead Americans on the Beach at Buna" by George Strock, and even that had to be accompanied by a truly remarkable full-page editorial.[186] The photograph, said John Dower, was "initially withheld from release under the official US policy of accentuating the positive and not showing graphic images of dead or gravely injured Americans. Publication of this and similar stark images marked the formal end of such censorship."[187] But remarkably, Karl Kae Knecht had taken the decision, backed by his editor at the *Courier*, to draw dead Americans in a front-page cartoon less than three months into the war. It can never be known, but perhaps they themselves asked the questions later spelled out in the famous *Life* editorial: "Here lie three Americans. What shall we say of them? Shall we say that this is a noble sight? Shall we say that this is a fine thing, that they should give their lives for their country? Or shall we say that this is too horrible to look at?…And so here it is. This is the reality that lies behind the names that come to rest at last on monuments in the leafy squares of busy American towns."[188] Cartoons and photographs are different, of course, but both are powerful. Long before it was officially sanctioned, Knecht offered his audience the ugly and bloody reality that lay behind the names on handsome and serene monuments.

The next three cartoons are comments on the end of war in Europe and the Pacific. His "A Nation That Followed a Book of Hate" appeared in the paper on May 4, 1945. Berlin had fallen at the beginning of the month, and Hitler's death was reported the previous day. Hitler's *Mein Kampf* lies in the foreground, torn to shreds. A skull and a bone lie beside it, and in the distance are enormous piles of human skulls and an infinite number of graves. A single blasted, leafless tree still stands, and in the smoke-filled sky fly carrion-eating birds. In perhaps the darkest comment he ever has her make, Kay sees only "Disaster, Destruction, Desolation, Degradation, [and] Death."[189] In the words of Craig Yoe, "It is hard to decide whether documentary photographs of war's human destruction are more gut-wrenching, or the graphic cartoonists' poignant pen and ink

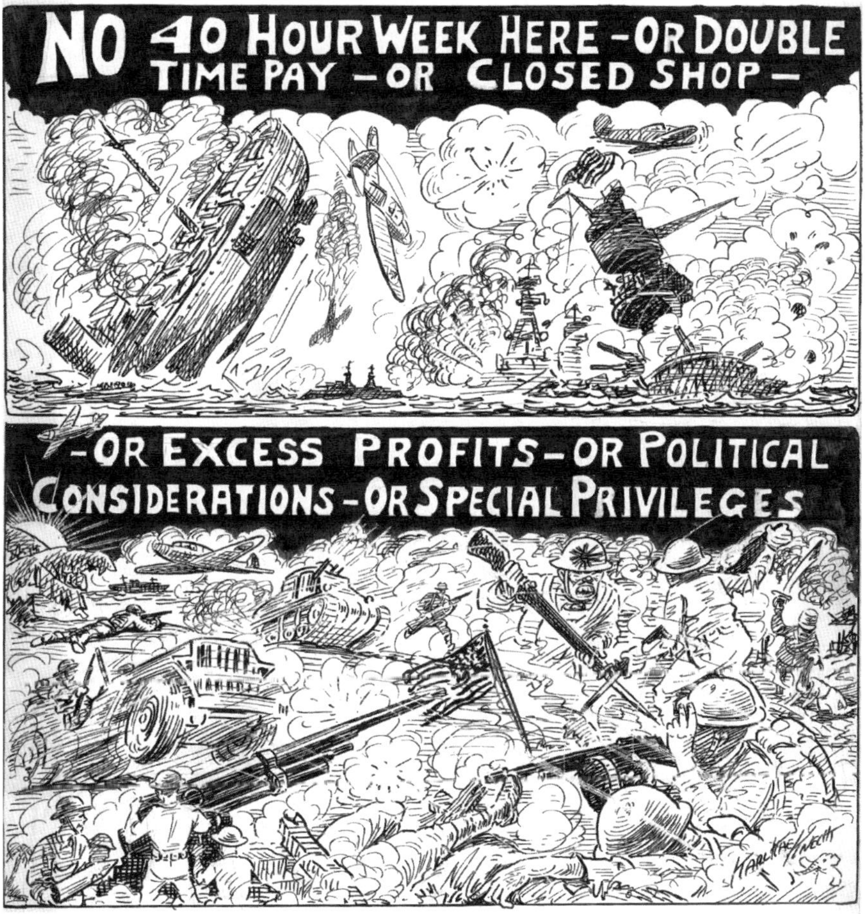

"While They Go Through All Hell's Fire—and More," March 20, 1942. *UE/EVPL.*

tableaus are. There are different ways to look at the same terror, uniting in the same conclusion: War is Hell."[190] Knecht told his audience many things over the years, but in this cartoon, he told them unambiguously that war was hell. The war is over, but there is no hint of celebration here—just regret and loss.

His reaction to the atomic bomb attack on Hiroshima was published on August 7, 1945. Captioned "Better Fold Up or Be Blown Up," it shows the bomb about to land on a racially stereotyped Japanese officer who is "folding up" the island that he is on. The smiling sun says that the bomb is made of "the stuff I'm powered with" while the bomb itself says that it is "the equal of 20,000 tons of TNT." A grim-faced Kay is in a boat close to Japan and reports that the bomb is two thousand times more powerful than any previous explosive. There is a gleeful and celebratory tone to the cartoon that seems incongruous today, but it has to be read in the context of a population that was tired of the deprivations of war, certain of the savage brutishness of the enemy, convinced of the legitimacy of the target and sure that there were no alternatives other than a hugely costly invasion of the Japanese homeland. The *Evansville Courier* spoke in an editorial on August 11, 1945, of "the intense satisfaction Americans feel over the destruction wrought in Hiroshima by the first atomic bomb....It is frightening as well as exhilarating to be the possessor of a weapon of such terrifying power, even though it is being used, at the moment, on an enemy who deserves no better fate."[191] Knecht's cartoon here is merely a visual representation of that view.

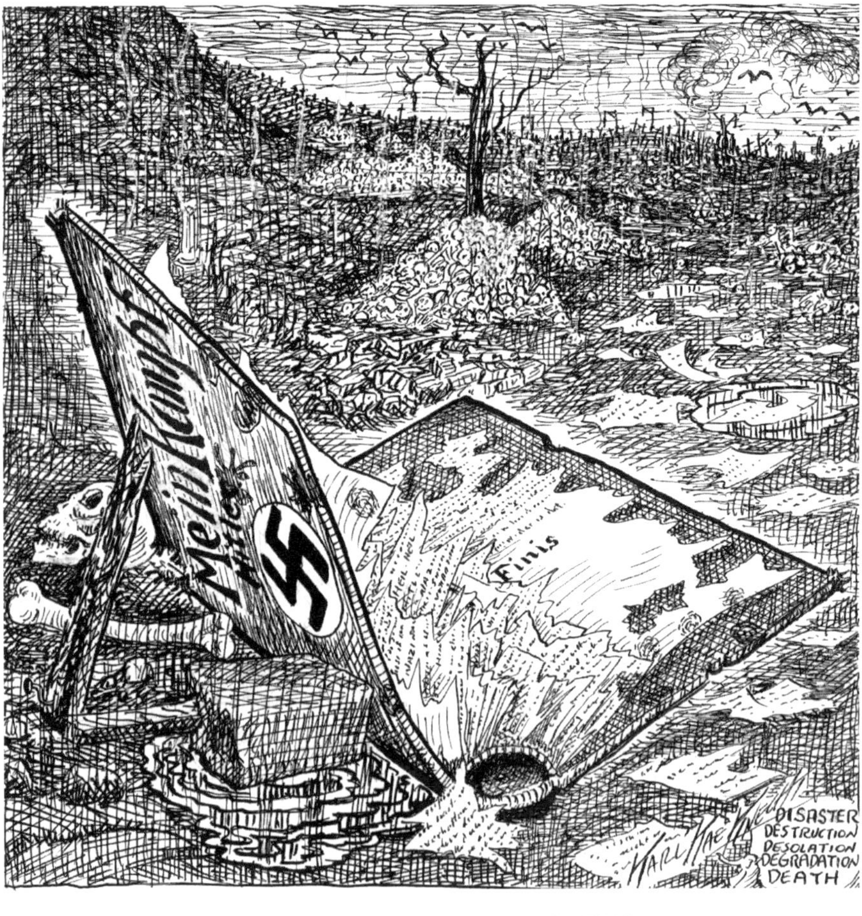

"A Nation That Followed a Book of Hate," May 4, 1945. *UE/EVPL.*

The third end-of-the-war cartoon is Knecht's reaction to the formal Japanese surrender aboard the USS *Missouri* in Tokyo Bay, published on September 1, 1945. While it is a powerful record of a hugely important symbolic moment, it is again a strikingly jovial, celebratory image, with strong overtones of the same racist stereotyping discussed earlier. The Japanese he draws are squinting, small and bucktoothed, rendered as scowling child-like figures in ostentatious uniforms, heavy with decorations and medals. The Allied representatives are tall, noble and heroic, smiling and proud at the moment of victory. Kay salutes and raises her trunk in triumph. The document is signed on the barrel of a naval gun rather than on the sober table that was actually used. Again, while it does not sit very comfortably with a modern audience, it is a reflection of the

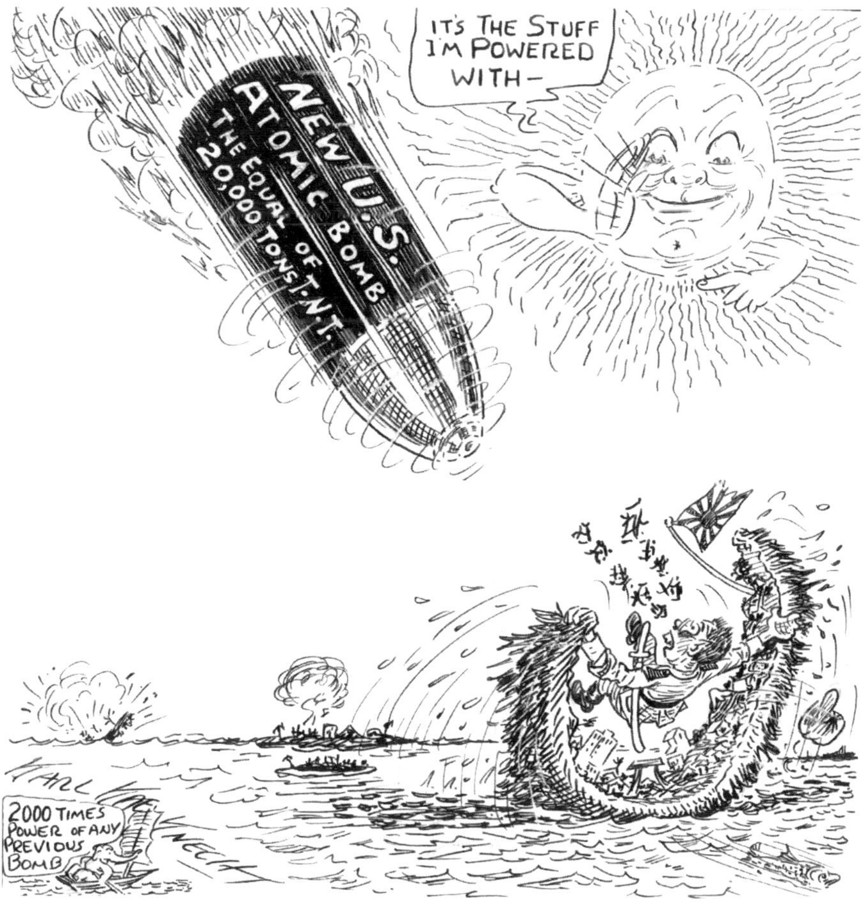

The atomic bomb falls on Japan, August 7, 1945. *UE/EVPL.*

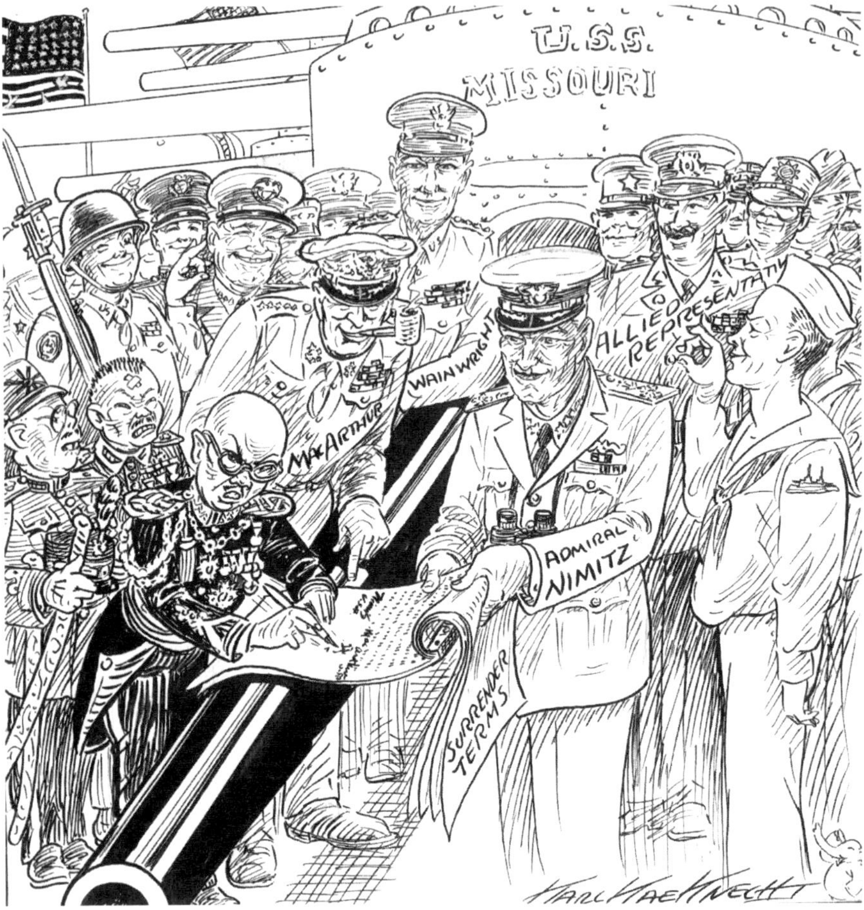

Japanese surrender is signed, September 1, 1945. UE/*EVPL*.

profound sense of the total nature of the Allied victory—it was, after all, an "unconditional surrender." It is also very much an American victory in this picture—all the named characters are American, although in reality eight of the ten Allied signatures on the surrender document were non-American. Again, this cartoon needs to be read carefully in the context of its time, and to condemn its self-righteousness, triumphalism and racism is perhaps to be anachronistic.

The final cartoon in this section, from August 6, 1945, is a really fine demonstration of his considerable talents as a caricaturist. Knecht here reflects on the just concluded Potsdam Conference, a meeting that has been called "a crucial turning point in modern history."[192] At it, the

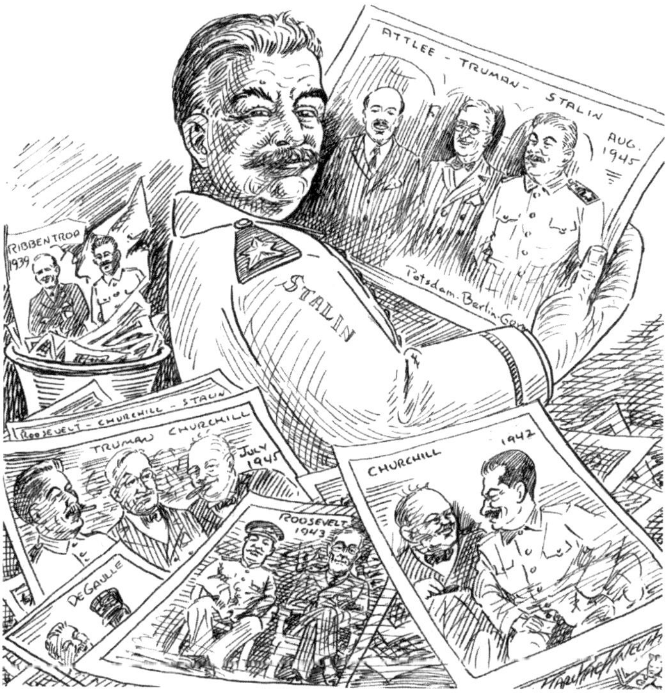

Stalin is depicted as the great survivor, August 6, 1945. *UE/EVPL.*

Allied leaders met to decide the fate of a remade world, but what Knecht comments on here is that the only Allied leader to have been present at every one of these leaders' conferences from beginning to end of the Alliance was Joseph Stalin. Roosevelt had died at Warm Springs, Georgia, on April 12, 1945, and Churchill was defeated in the British general election, the stunning results of which were declared on July 26, leaving the Soviet dictator as the last man standing. Knecht records Stalin's meetings with various Allied leaders at the Moscow Conferences (1942 and 1944), Tehran (1943), Yalta (February 1945) and Potsdam (July–August 1945). There is a picture of Stalin and German foreign minister Ribbentrop in the trashcan—a humorous bookend to his "Bear Hug" cartoon discussed earlier. He captures all of the leaders very effectively in this image, which is both an interesting historical commentary and a fine example of his ability to capture the physical essence of famous figures.

Having considered a number of his cartoons that focused on the war abroad, it is now time to look at the work that he did that focused on the homefront. Evansville was a truly remarkable place during the war, with a workforce that grew by tens of thousands, producing by the end of the war billions of bullets, thousands of airplanes and hundreds of oceangoing ships, as well as numerous other items both large and small. In the words of Patrick Wathen, what was done in the city was "nothing short of outstanding."[193] In examining Knecht's wartime cartoons, it emerges that he covered virtually the whole range of homefront activities in Evansville, and what is fascinating is that it is possible to find evidence that the activism of many of these cartoons really did have an effect. Knecht received complimentary letters from, among others, the director of the Office of War Mobilization and Reconversion (future treasury secretary John Snyder), the Office of Defense Transportation, the State of Indiana Alcoholic Beverage Commission, the Belgian Red Cross in New York, the Office of Price Administration and even from the City of Evansville Rat Control Program Committee. In October 1944, the administrator of the Office of Price Administration, Chester Bowles, wrote a letter to the editor of the *Courier* to express thanks for "the fine work your paper has done in supporting the OPA programs," mentioning specifically Knecht's cartoons. He also received grateful letters from Edward Stettinius Jr., U.S. secretary of state and first U.S. ambassador to the United Nations.[194]

A fine specific example of this is "There is a War Going On," published on June 5, 1944. It is another very stark cartoon that contrasts a large group of women playing bingo, along with several more who are playing cards, with a wounded and possibly dying soldier in a foxhole who does not have the bandages that he needs. One of the soldiers is talking about the fact that the "local Red Cross chapter is appealing for volunteer workers to make bandages to send over for us at war." This is in reference to the fact that in Evansville hundreds of local women volunteered with the Red Cross, making tens of thousands of surgical dressings, but more volunteers were always needed. It clearly had a real-life effect, as a couple of days later, Knecht received the following letter on Red Cross notepaper: "My dear Mr. Knecht, Thanks very much for your drawing in Monday's *Courier* on behalf of surgical dressings. The telephone buzzed all day Monday as a result of the publicity and we had new workers come in. I do not know whether they were Bingo players or not. I certainly appreciate your interest, and do not know how we could exist without it. Sincerely, Aline E. Igleheart."[195]

Knecht drew numerous cartoons in support of the sale of war bonds, basically year-round but with more emphasis when there was a war bond drive being pushed particularly hard. A great example, printed on May 21, 1945, was published in support of the Seventh War Loan Drive. Captioned "Come On, Help Put Us Over," it shows Uncle Sam, whose eyes are on the viewer, raising a gigantic number seven that is about to become a bridge to Japan. The Japanese leader, bespectacled and bucktoothed as always, is urging his followers to fight to the death but does not see what is coming. Kay leaps up and down in enthusiastic encouragement. Knecht had also drawn cartoons supporting this drive on both of the previous two days. On May 23, the chair of the Vanderburgh County War Finance Committee, Mike Schaeffer, wrote to him to say, "We truly appreciate the wonderful cooperation you are giving us in your cartoons during the Seventh War Loan. We have had any number of comments which show that people are really getting the messages as you intended. I ran across one this morning."[196] It is almost impossible to quantify the effect of a cartoon most times, but these two examples show that there is evidence that Knecht's cartoons hit their mark during World War II.

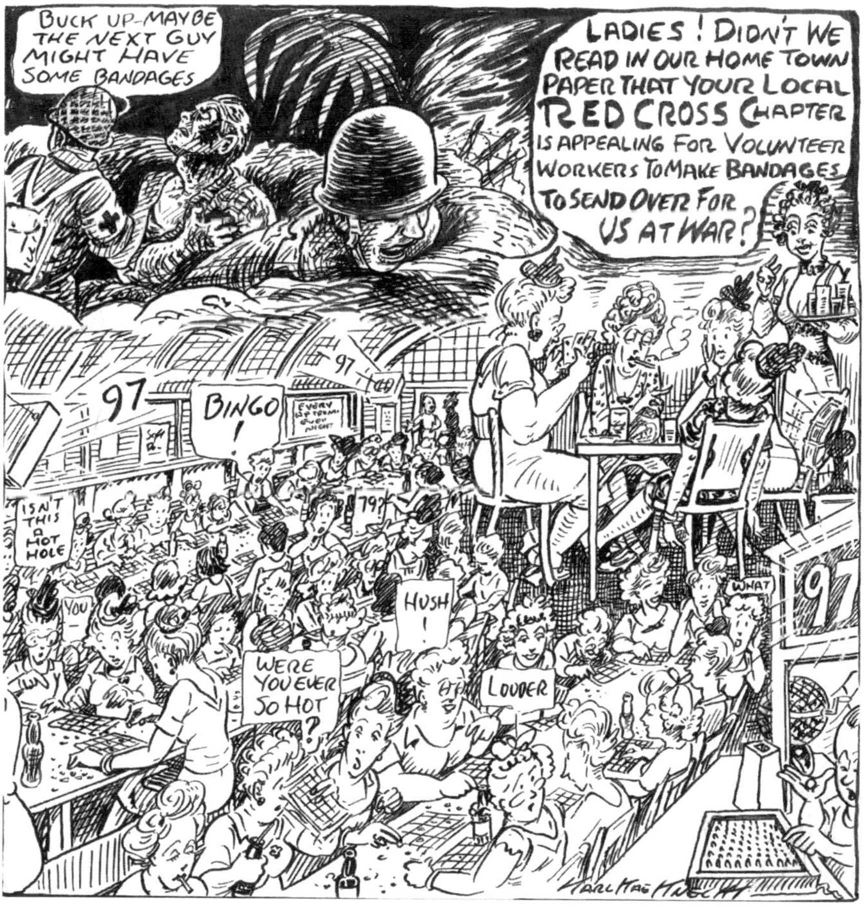

"There Is a War Going On," June 5, 1944. *UE/EVPL.*

Knecht was an activist for other fundraising efforts, too, of course. On October 27, 1943, he drew a cartoon for Navy Day, captioned "Another of Our Days." At the top, a wonderfully drawn navy battleship fires a salvo of thanks to Evansville while Mr. Public, pushing an "LST Built in Evansville" down the launching ways, responds, "You're Welcome." The iconic Southern Indiana Gas and Electric Company station is visible in the background of the launch, though it should be noted that the LST is being launched much faster than it would have been in reality; Knecht must have known this, having been a launching platform guest of honor at the launch of LST 123 in August 1943.[197] In the end, the city would produce 167 LSTs, more than any other inland shipyard in the country; in 1944, Evansville would launch an astounding average of 1 ship every four days, and Knecht drew many cartoons honoring the work of the Evansville Shipyard.[198] "US Public" beams down, saluting. The bottom half of the cartoon features Mr. Public yet again, fairly sternly enjoining the readers to contribute to the Evansville Community War Chest Fund while a war plant worker places his pledge in the box.

The shipyard is the focus of another powerful cartoon that appeared on August 24, 1942. It was a fine drawing of a ship being built, with a welder in goggles and visor waving in the foreground. Three cranes are visible, as is an Army-Navy Excellence flag. But this is also another example of Knecht's pedagogical instincts, using the cartoon to inform his audience about Indiana's significant contributions to the U.S. Navy. The ship being built is turned into a map of Indiana to highlight the "plants, depots, training schools, [and] camps" that are in the state, as well as a Naval Air Squadron and inland shipyards. Places like Gary, Burns City, Newport, Peru, Fort Wayne and Jeffersonville (a river city that, like Evansville, built LSTs) are all marked. In one of her more mysterious remarks, Kay rows her boat and mentions the "the salt air."[199]

Women played an enormous role in Indiana's war effort, and by 1943, they made up about half of the workforce in the state's war plants; at Evansville's Chrysler Ordnance Plant, for example, 60 percent of the workers were women.[200] In a cartoon published on February 3, 1943, captioned "Plenty of Jobs Open," Knecht summed up not just the contribution of female war workers but also that of women in uniform. He was an enthusiastic proponent of women in the war effort, here celebrating all of the various acronyms that represented the different branches of service, such as the WAACs, the WAVES, the WAMS and the WAFS. He points out that "women in service release men

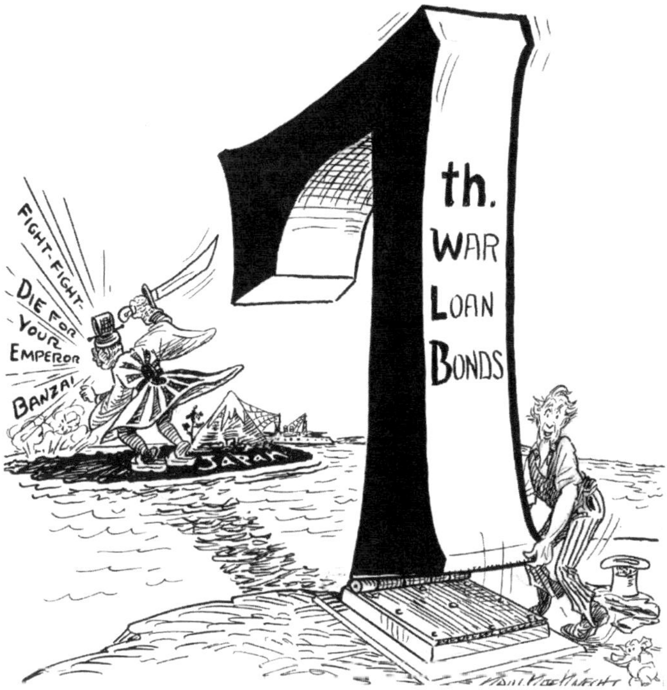

The seventh war loan, May 21, 1945. UE/*EVPL*.

for combat" and then in the bottom right of the cartoon, he draws a wonderful version of a "Rosie the Riveter," tools sticking out of her back pocket, declaring that she and women like her are the "WOWS"—"Women of Work Shops." It is a powerful document of the reality of homefront America, where the war effort simply could not have been sustained without the contributions of millions of women in all parts of the economy and the military.

Knecht, like almost everyone else, was deeply concerned with security in wartime. Evansville, with such a large number of war plants, was considered to be a target for enemy espionage, and complicated security measures were taken. In June 1942, F.M. McWhirter, the navy's district security officer, wrote to the manager of the shipyard: "The danger of espionage and sabotage to all facilities producing war material is ever-present. Your shipyard is vital to the success of the whole war effort. It must produce without interruption. A well-planned and maintained security program is the only possible defense against possible devastating enemy action."[201] Knecht also believed in the importance of urging care when speaking—loose lips, after all, could sink ships[202]—and, in fact, one of his most memorable, simple, striking and humorous cartoons was on this topic, published on July 27, 1942. The

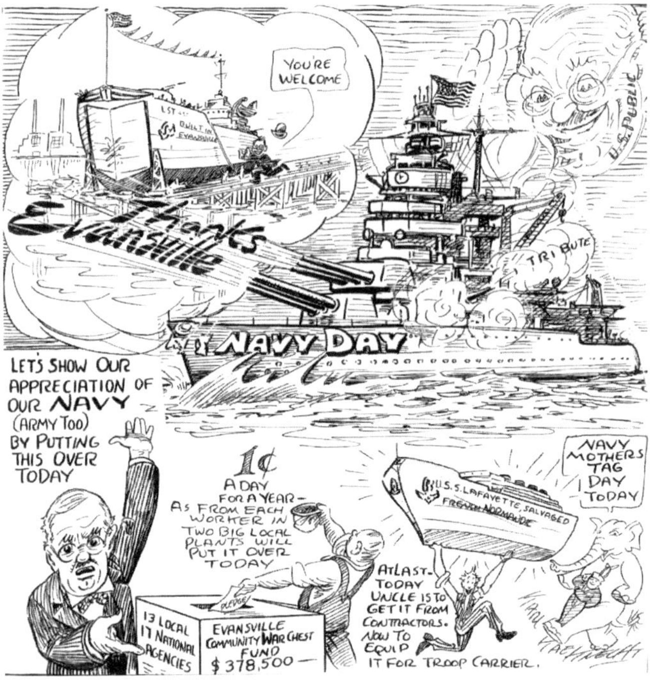

The celebration of Navy Day, October 27, 1943. *UE/EVPL.*

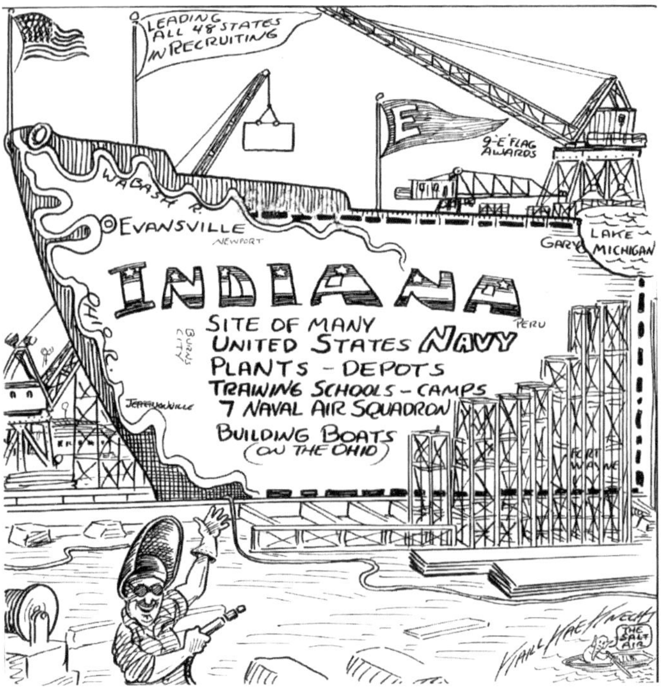

Indiana's war effort, August 24, 1942. *UE/EVPL.*

cartoon had the caption "Remember—Might Be in an Ear Near You," and it showed an ear with tiny representations of Hirohito, Mussolini and Hitler peeping out, with their hands cupped behind their own ears. It almost goes without saying that the Japanese figure is a racist stereotype, but all three of the Axis figures are objects of ridicule. While it is making a serious point, that enemy spies might be able to hear any conversation even in little old Evansville, it was also designed to offer comfort to the readers by mocking and belittling the Axis powers.

In the middle of 1942, the war was going badly for the Allies at every turn—in western Europe, in the Soviet Union, in North Africa, in the Pacific Islands and in the Atlantic Ocean. Morale was dangerously low,

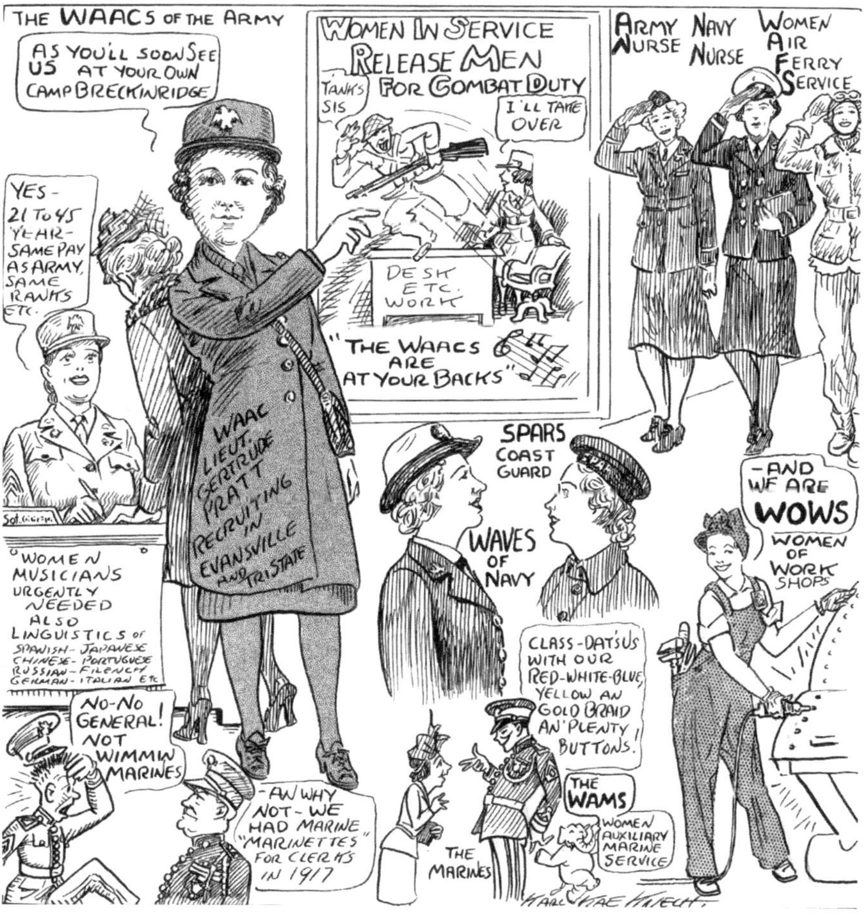

Female war workers, February 3, 1943. *UE/EVPL.*

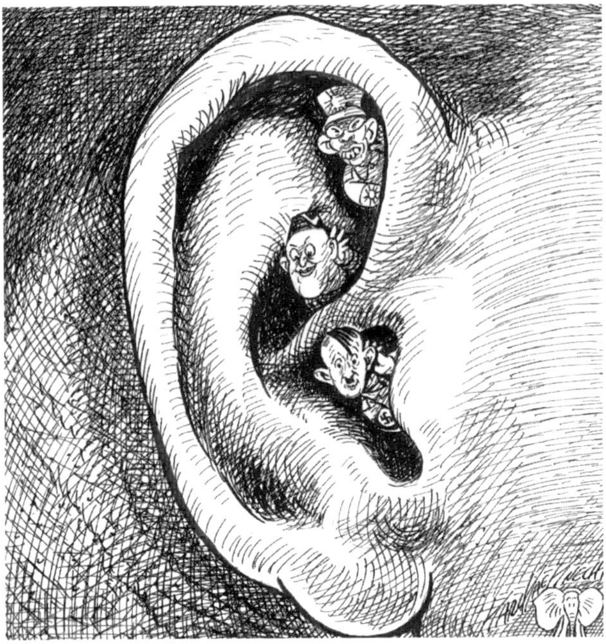

"Remember—Might Be in an Ear Near You," July 27, 1942. *UE/EVPL*.

as people were forced to read bad news on the front page of the *Courier* day in and day out. But on seeing this image, it is easy to imagine a citizen of Evansville getting the message about being careful about loose lips while also getting a chuckle at the expense of the most terrifying figures on the planet. It is hard to fear someone that you are laughing at,[203] and so Karl Kae Knecht here manages to achieve two vital objectives with one elegant drawing.

The final homefront cartoon appeared on July 24, 1943. In contrast to the previous cartoon, this appeared at a time when things seemed to be going much better for the Allies on virtually every front. This lent urgency to the cartoon, captioned "No Time to Slow Down—Work Harder Than Ever." A paper trumpets, "Allied Successes, Africa, Sicily…Russians Rout Germans" while a group of war plant workers stand around reading papers, gossiping and applying makeup. A piece of machinery, labeled "War Work," is inactive, with spider webs developing on either side. Into this scene of slothful inertia is interposed a soldier, with one foot on the battlefield, hitting a worker with the butt of his rifle while pointing out that "it's far from won." Kay adds her view that there is "a long, long way to go." It is a very strong statement—Knecht here almost plays the part of the Old Testament prophet, wagging his boney finger in the face of a lazy

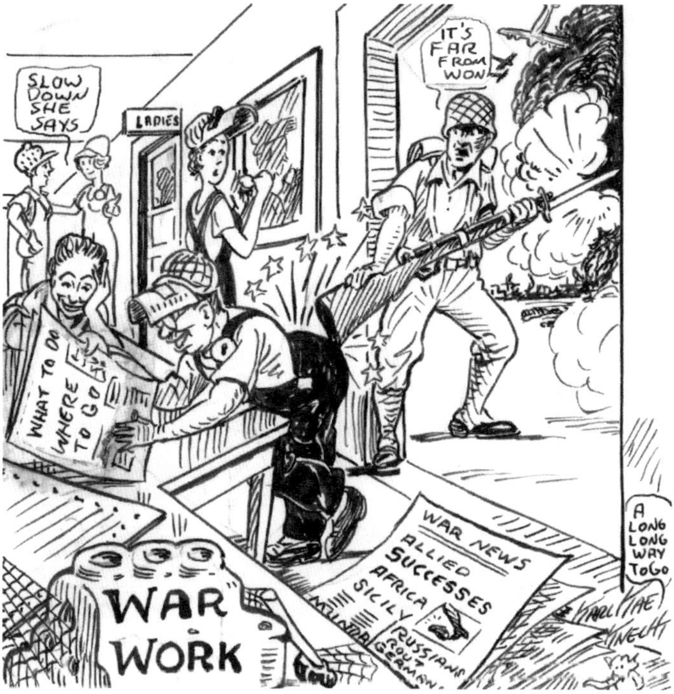

The war is far from won, July 24, 1943. *UE/EVPL.*

and complacent public. And it is an effective cartoon precisely because he was such a trusted figure, one who was with his readers every step of the war, telling hard truths while still encouraging and cajoling and amusing along the way.

Between 1941 and 1945, Knecht drew cartoons on one grand subject—World War II—almost every single day. It serves to communicate to a modern observer just how remarkably omnipresent the war was in people's minds. People who were in Evansville during the war confirm today how much this was true, but sometimes it has to be seen to be believed. Karl Kae Knecht never wore a uniform during the war—he turned sixty in 1943—but his patriotic activism served a truly vital purpose. Reminding his readers of the stakes, urging them to participate, informing them about events, pressing them to give money and then give more money and, above all, encouraging them to continue with the fight, Knecht helped the people of Evansville do their part in winning the most important war in human history.

Chapter 6

CARTOONS 1946–60

While World War II was an extremely significant event, the new world that it ushered in was certainly not lacking in momentous incidents and developments. As Karl Kae Knecht progressed toward the twilight of his cartooning career, he was able to grapple with some of the most pressing issues of the twentieth century. This final chapter will move in a mostly chronological manner through this era, analyzing eleven of his most interesting cartoons from these fourteen years on topics ranging from race relations to the bomb and from the space race to political correctness. It is obvious that this was also the period when his drawing style reached its peak—the marriage of the techniques he was using and the printing technology available leading to a series of images that are extremely pleasing to the eye. In the words of Phil Ensley, "Such mastery requires years to achieve; that he did achieve it is obvious to those who followed his cartoons through the years."[204]

Race relations have haunted the United States since before it even existed, and they haunt the country to this day. As has been seen, Knecht himself was not immune to the effect of race in his art, and both Indiana in general and Evansville in particular had experienced the complex and usually negative repercussions of racism. In 1946, Evansville was still basically segregated, and as recently as 1930, one of the most notorious lynchings in American history took place not far away in Marion, Indiana.[205] The Ku Klux Klan had been enormously influential in Indiana in the early 1920s, and between 1922 and 1924 in Evansville and Vanderburgh County, it became, according to Leonard Moore, "a local sensation and a political force that was powerful enough to unseat the district's anti-Klan Democratic congressman. Eventually, more than 5,400 men—or 23 percent of all native white men in the county—joined the Evansville Klan." D.C. Stephenson, the notorious Klan leader who once said, "I am the law in Indiana," was ultimately to become the grand dragon of the state. He was one of the most powerful Klansmen in the nation, and he lived in Evansville.[206]

The Klan collapsed in the mid-'20s, partly as a result of the conviction of Stephenson for the brutal kidnapping, rape and torture of a young woman, but in the 1940s, it was showing signs of revival. The first cartoon in this chapter was published on June 1, 1946, under the caption "Stop Him Before He Gets Going." It was a piece of activism in response to the revival of the Klan in Georgia in May 1946, which the *Evansville Press* described: "Fiery crosses atop historic Stone Mountain near here last night heralded the Dixie rebirth of the Ku Klux Klan on a theme of 'white supremacy.' More than 700 white-hooded figures assembled on the torch-lighted, wind-swept granite mound…[where] oil torches placed in niches formed a burning cross 300 feet high and 165 feet wide visible for miles."[207] Knecht's message is unequivocal, supporting two of the methods that ultimately crippled the Klan in the 1940s,

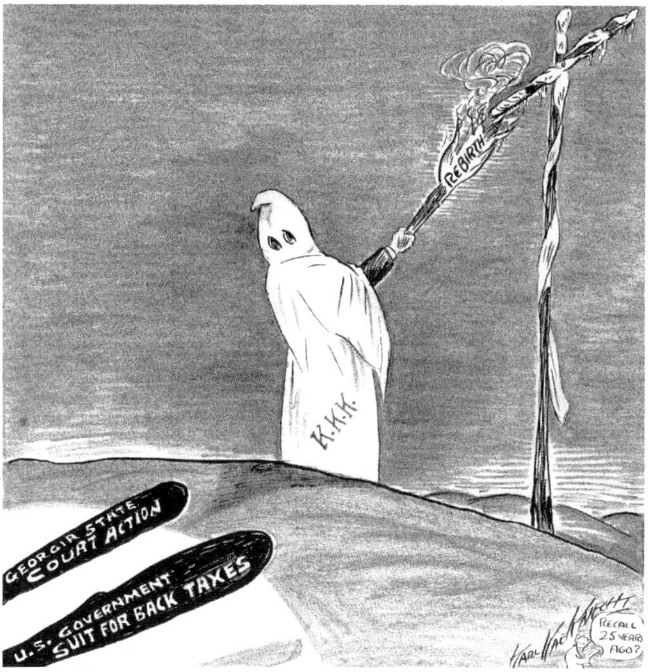

Fighting the Ku Klux Klan, June 1, 1946. *UE/EVPL.*

"Georgia State Court Action" and a "US Government Suit for Back Taxes," which here appear as police nightsticks. Kay turns and asks the reader if they "recall 25 years ago?"—a challenging reference to the rise of the Klan in the early 1920s in Indiana and especially in Evansville itself.

The second image is a fabulous caricature of Harry Truman with the sword of Damocles hanging over him, published on May 17, 1947, and captioned "There It Hangs." He is about to either sign or veto a "Labor Law" from Congress, and the sword is labeled "He will be damned if he does and damned if he does not." This cartoon represents a pivotal moment in the struggle between organized labor and business, as it is discussing the Labor-Management Relations Act of 1947, more usually called the Taft-Hartley Act. This act was motivated by Republican hostility to the New Deal, a fear of the power of unions, and the prevailing and growing antagonism to communism. It was basically an attack on the unions and their ability to organize by the Republican House and Senate that had been elected in 1946: "It weakened unions in American life, while enhancing forces resisting unionization."[208] Truman had not been a "particularly prolabor" senator but took the decision to veto this act, calling it a "slave labor" law. The cartoon captures Truman's dilemma, realizing that if he were to sign the law, he would lose the support of the ten million members of organized labor but if he vetoed it, he would be seen to be going against a Congress that had been elected in a Republican landslide the previous November.[209] The *Courier* was generally a pro-business newspaper, and while Knecht supported the little man in many ways, he was also very much an enemy of activist unions and usually criticized strikes. This cartoon, however, is focused on the loneliness of the man in power, the man who has to make the tough decisions; it does not in itself take a position on the act but instead concentrates on the solitary figure of Truman, who must make the decision one way or the other. Labor relations have been a fraught part of human history almost forever, and in the postwar era in the United States, they were a critical area of conflict; this cartoon, while not taking sides, does manage to illustrate the enormity and the complexity of the issue.

Another issue that has transfixed American politics for virtually the entire postwar period is relations with Israel, and Knecht made his position clear in May 1948 with a drawing that was captioned "When a 'Feller' Really Needs a Friend." It depicts the "10 day old Jewish State" as a simple shepherd boy in a short tunic and sandals. He is being savagely dragged to the ground by the "Arabs of Palestine," who simultaneously grasp his bruised arm and pull his hair; at the same time, a military figure representing Egypt strikes him on the

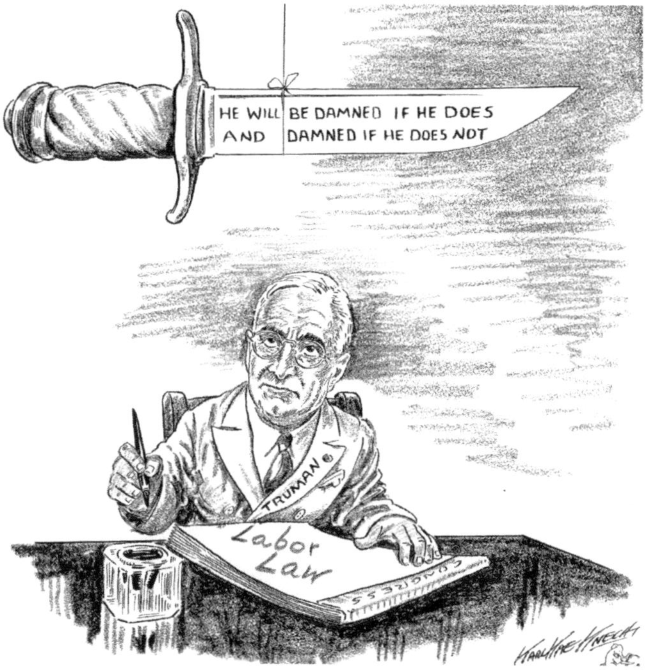

Truman and the sword of Damocles, May 17, 1947. *UE/EVPL.*

head with a heavy club. Behind this is a huge throng, including Syria, Lebanon, Transjordan and Saudi Arabia, armed with rifles and long curved sabers, rushing to join the attack on Israel. It is a comment on the events that followed the establishment of the State of Israel on May 14, 1948, when the Israelis were attacked by a coalition of Arab states.[210] Knecht unmistakably identifies Israel as the boy David of the Bible story—perhaps the most heroic underdog figure in the history of literature—and so makes his pro-Israel stance evident.

Interestingly, other than the traditional costumes and a possibly stereotypical Arab facial structure, there is an absence of the racism evident in some earlier depictions. But clearly Israel is the plucky little good guy (who, of course, will ultimately win), and Israel's enemies are the villains of the piece. Knecht's position on Israel was, however, a little complicated. Although a man who was sympathetic to Judaism, frequently noting events like the Jewish New Year and sometimes placing Hebrew phrases in his cartoons, Knecht had earlier been critical of the partition of Palestine, likening it to a camel that had been cut in two, leaving neither side viable.[211] Just a few days before his cartoon of Israel under attack, he drew one in which David (the UN) faced up to Goliath (war) in an apparent even-handed approach to the conflict. Despite the complexities and ambiguities of Middle East politics, on this day, at least, Knecht was on the side of Israel.

The Cold War was perhaps the most significant phenomenon in international (and often domestic) politics during this period, and Knecht drew many cartoons that dealt with it. On July 26, 1950, he drew a cartoon that has already been mentioned, recycling the gorilla-savage-beast trope but, this time, making the savage beast "communism" rather than Nazism. The setup and indeed the entire cartoon, especially the savage beast, are virtually identical to the earlier version. The timing of this cartoon is significant; in July 1950, the Korean War was not going well—the main front-page story that day reported, "Communist troops have loosed a lightning drive along Korea's south coast...overwhelming strategic Yougdoug and driving the American defenders two miles to the east."[212] The image is a really interesting example of how one decade's enemy of civilization gives way to another; if Knecht were alive today, perhaps he would be drawing the same beast but labeling it "Radicalized Islam."

Six years later, on February 3, 1956, he produced another notable Cold War cartoon that showed British prime minister Sir Anthony Eden shaking hands with President Eisenhower. It powerfully sets out the Western perspective on the entire Cold War, as Knecht contrasts the "slavery" of

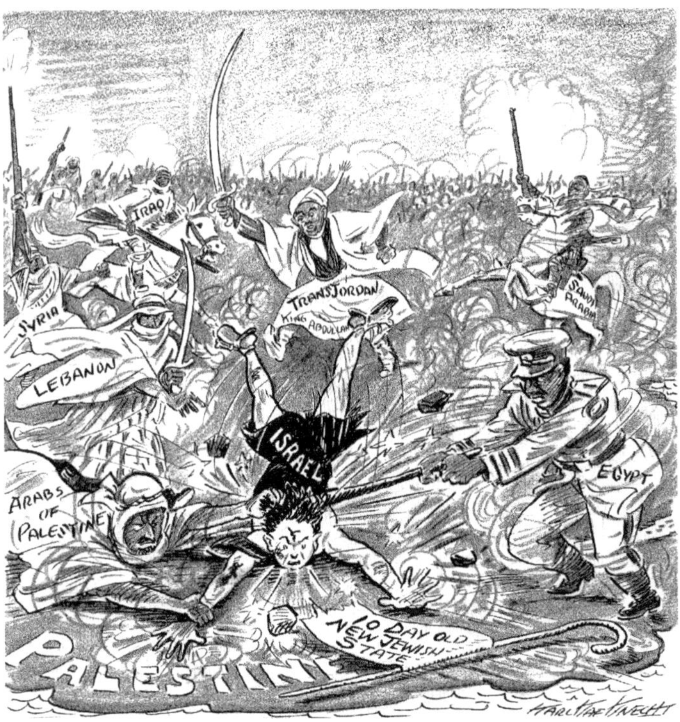

Israel is attacked by many enemies, May 1948. *UE/EVPL.*

communism, represented by a gigantic ball and chain, with the burning torch of "liberty." The central statement in the image is: "While Russia by Communistic aggression has taken freedom from 100,000,000 persons in ten countries—we have helped 600,000,000 in 20 countries to set up national freedom…" The year 1956 was to be one of the key years of the conflict, witnessing both the Suez Crisis and the Hungarian Revolution; Knecht's position on one of the most fundamental political divides of the twentieth century could not have been clearer.

One of the most important aspects of the Cold War was, of course, the nuclear arms race, and one of the most momentous steps in that race was the development of the hydrogen bomb in the early 1950s. In a cartoon of January 21, 1950, Knecht responds to the growing conversation in the country about the next technological step for nuclear weapons. The previous day, the paper had reported in a front-page story that "the Truman administration today was reported favorable to production of the hydrogen superbomb on which experimental work is already being pushed."[213] In a very powerful and telling cartoon, Mr. Public reacts with shock and horror to the news—his mouth is open, his eyes are wide and his hair stands on end. He absorbs the information that the new bomb is potentially "1000 times more ruinous" than the bombs that destroyed Hiroshima and Nagasaki, and Kay covers her ears. Unlike the cartoon that greeted the atomic bomb—which was light and cheerful and talked of its "power"—this one is dark and frightening and puts the emphasis on the destructive capabilities of the bomb, using the word "ruinous." Technology was evolving fast, and so was Knecht.

Having drawn Stalin at the Potsdam Conference as the great survivor of all the Allied war leaders, Knecht was to mark the Soviet dictator's death eight years later. This cartoon appeared on March 5, 1953, with the caption "For Better or for Worse?" It shows twelve hands reaching for the vacated power that Stalin left behind, but a lash and a bloody pointed cudgel symbolize the power; these two items combine to cast a shadow that is the Soviet symbol of the hammer and sickle. In a reminder of the challenges of drawing a daily cartoon when news changes from minute to minute, Knecht drew a note saying "Stalin unconscious from stroke," which is what the situation was as he drew, but also included a piece with the word "dead" on it that could have been literally cut and pasted onto the image to make it more up to date. Stalin did indeed die between the drawing being executed and its publication, although the cartoon was not changed. It appeared on the editorial page (as his cartoons did at this point) opposite an editorial that made clear the paper's

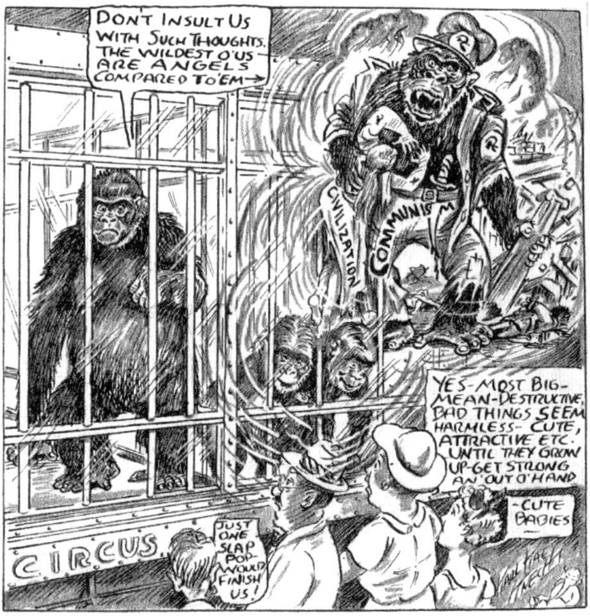

Communism is depicted as a gorilla, July 26, 1950. *UE/EVPL.*

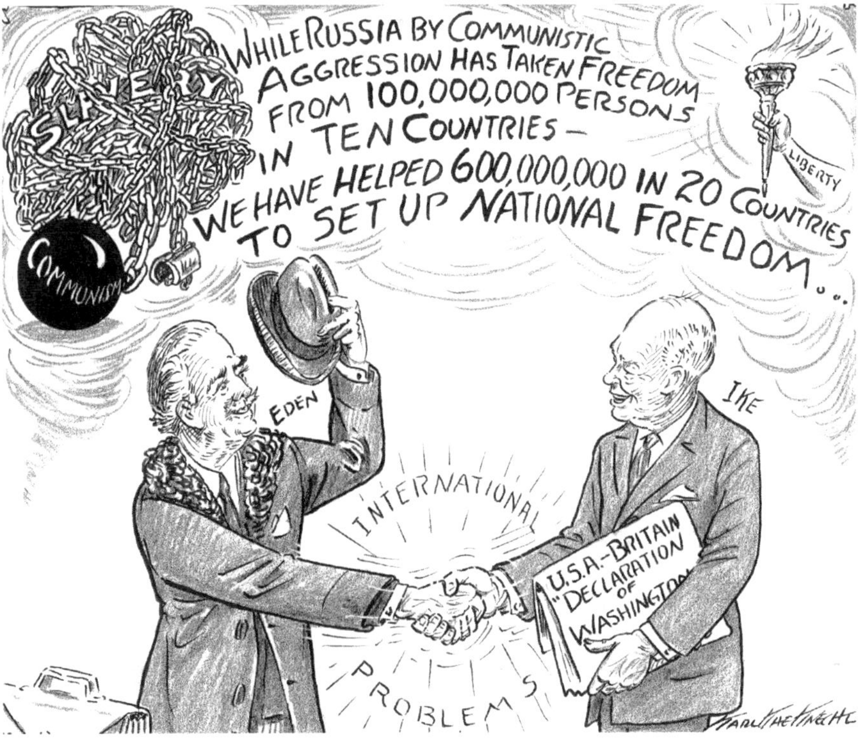

The slavery of Communism, February 3, 1956. *UE/EVPL.*

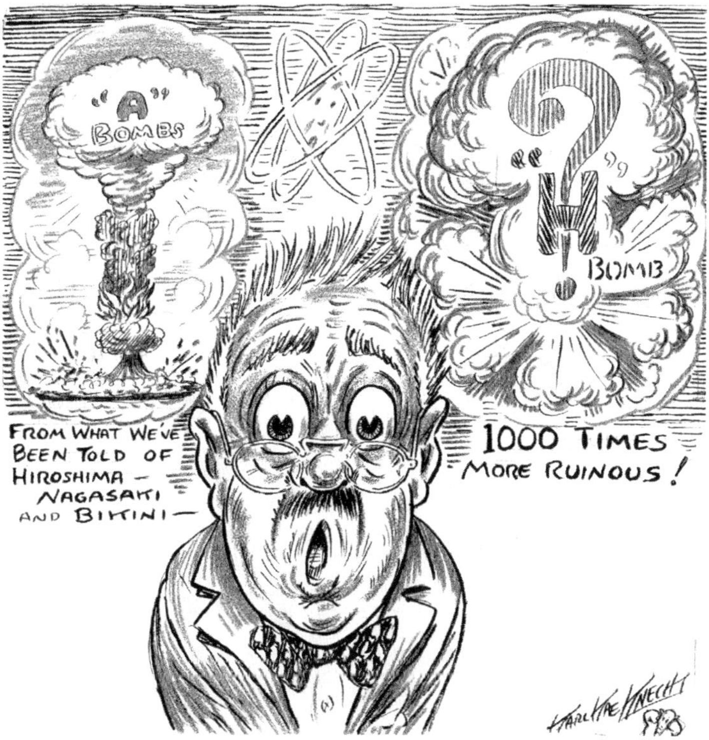

"Mr. Public" responds to the hydrogen bomb, January 21, 1950. *UE/EVPL.*

position, one that might well have exactly matched Knecht's own: "We of the free west stand in mortal danger today, as we stood yesterday and the day before, and will stand so long as the great power of Russia is ruled by communist totalitarians, bent on enslaving the whole world."[214]

Of course domestic politics continued its usual course, and from time to time, Evansville was visited by figures running for national office. One such event was marked by the cartoon of October 16, 1956, that depicts in Knecht's unique style the visit of Vice President Richard Nixon to the city. Nixon was the running mate of Dwight Eisenhower in the 1956 presidential election and is here depicted flying into the airport and then proceeding on a motorcade through Evansville. He is accompanied by his wife, Pat, and the Republican candidate for Congress, D. Bailey Merrill, who has apparently autographed this original. It is in many ways an archetypal Knecht cartoon, with high-energy, bold, confident caricatures, a history lesson in the form of a reminiscence about the "old whistle-stop train trips by candidates," wonderfully accurate renderings of Evansville landmarks, including the old courthouse and the college and, of course, the presence of Mr. Public and Kay. Kay appears twice, making her usual comment in the corner but also running alongside the motorcade. It is a wonderful document of a moment in American electoral history and of an exciting day in Evansville.[215]

The next cartoon, a series of detailed images that look more like a strip cartoon, demonstrates Knecht's ability to put current events into an historical context and to react to world events as a spokesman not just of one country but of the human race. It was published on November 6, 1957, just two days after the launch by the Soviets of *Sputnik 1*, the first man-made satellite. This was, of course, a significant blow in the Cold War space race, and the *Courier* editorial that appeared alongside the cartoon was full of alarm and foreboding, stating, "The capacity of Russian science was underestimated. Sputnik should now cause Americans to realize that the creative and cultural resources of this country could be much better used than they are, and that we should not make easy assumptions of superiority."[216] Knecht could easily have gone down that road, too, but instead, he chose to deliver one of his beautiful and cheerful history lessons, on "Man's Gaze Skyward." He put Sputnik into the context of man's instinct to reach for the skies, tracing the history of manned

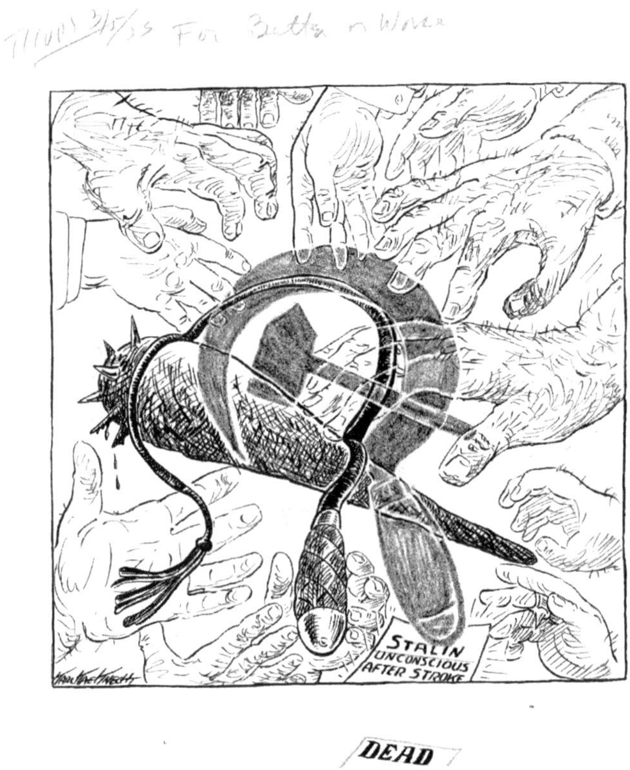

Stalin's death, March 5, 1953. *UE/EVPL.*

flight with a series of intricate drawings of balloons, dirigibles and airships [slipping in a glimpse of the Evansville skyline, of course], early airplanes, jets and finally "man-made satellites." At the end, Mr. Public turns to the audience, binoculars in hand, and shows them a map with times when Sputnik can be seen. Far from parochial or nationalistic anxieties, this cartoon demonstrates Knecht's infectious enthusiasm for flight, for progress, and for human endeavor. With the caption, "What Next!!," he is not just looking back but looking forward, excitedly contemplating a brave new world where man's limits no longer lie on this planet alone.

A very different side of the late-career Knecht is shown in the next cartoon, which is from June 13, 1959, just months before his retirement. Although drawn almost sixty years ago, its savage attack on the concept of politically correct speech would appeal to a certain part of the community today. It is funny, on one level, but it is also extremely harsh, especially by

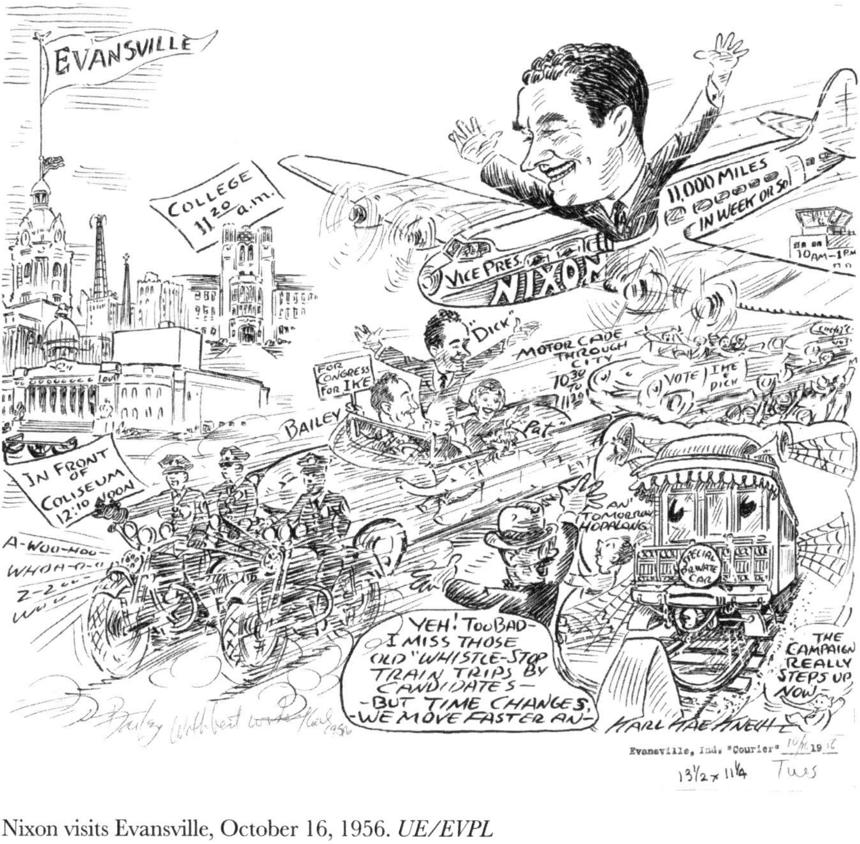

Nixon visits Evansville, October 16, 1956. *UE/EVPL*

Knecht's standards. Above the caption "Do Not Expect All Adults to Be Sensible!" it shows a "Racial Fanatic"—drawn in an extremely pejorative way—who is stripping children's books of their beloved characters because of the supposed racial offence that they cause. A black sheep, a black pig, Black Beauty, Mary's Little Lamb and the Little Red Hen are all being dismissed for the sin of having colors associated with their characters. Two bemused and disappointed children observe the scene, and at the top is a "Notice" that announces a ban on "imitations or impersonations, straight or in burlesque, of any and all races, [and] nationalities…in jokes, cartoons, stories." Given what has been said already on the subject of the use of racial stereotypes in cartoons, including Knecht's, and the prevalence of "Sambo" in almost every conceivable form of expression, this cartoon seems uncomfortably like a last defiant gesture from an old world that is facing a terrifying new reality. A white patriarchy had ruled the United

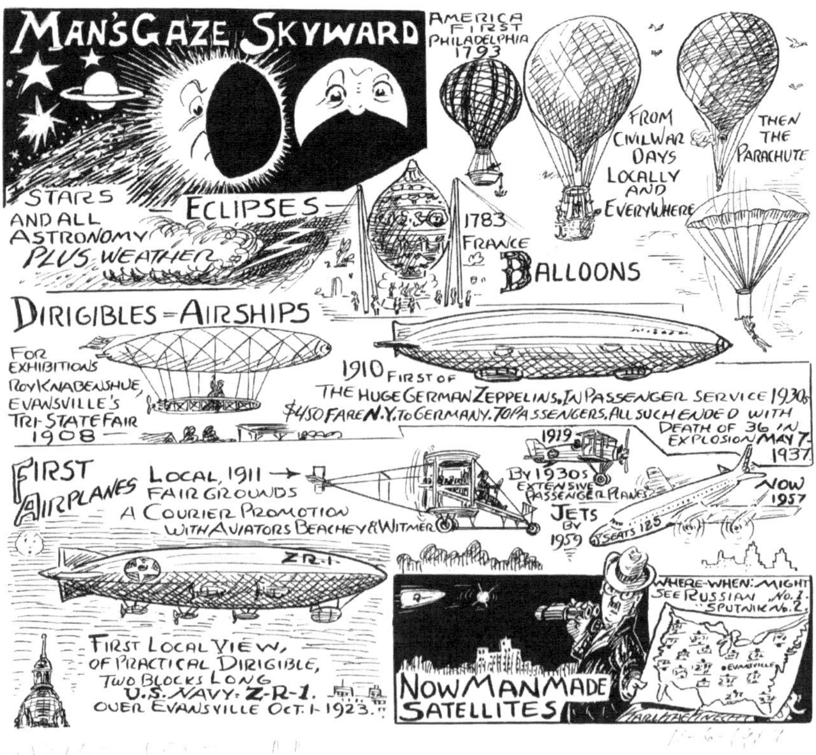

Sputnik and the history of air travel, November 6, 1957. *UE/EVPL.*

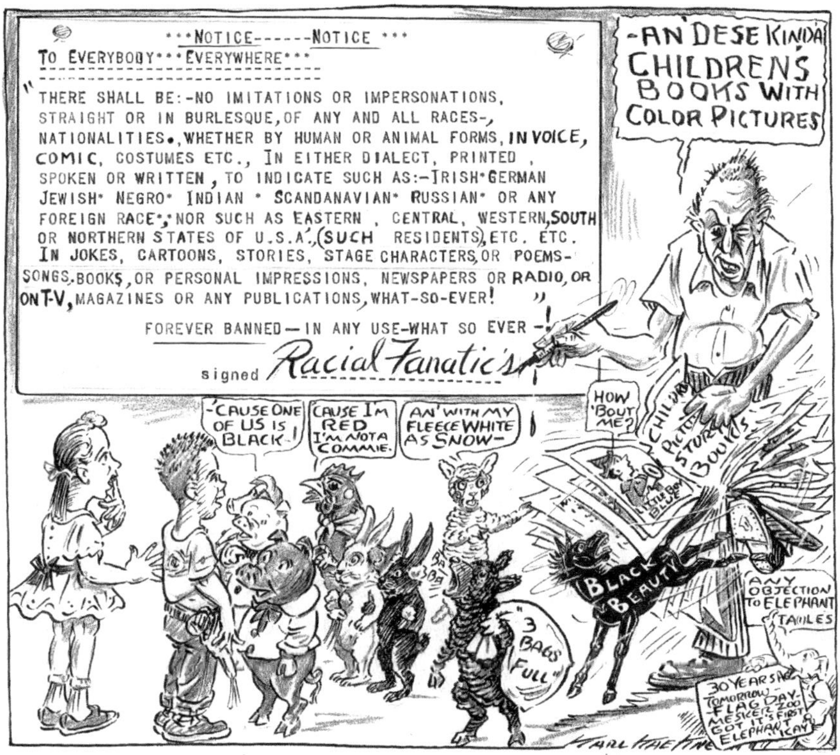

Racial political correctness is condemned, June 13, 1959. *UE/EVPL.*

States since the day it was born, but in 1959, change was coming. The 1960s were but a year away. The civil rights movement had begun, the feminist movement was beginning, Elvis Presley was shaking his hips, the men who would be the Beatles were playing music together and Bob Dylan had started playing small concerts. The times they were a-changin', and from the evidence of this cartoon, Karl Kae Knecht did not much like what he saw.

Knecht drew cartoons dealing with all the issues, great and small, of the postwar world, but he never forgot his role as an activist for his own community. The final cartoon of this chapter, from November 12, 1958, reminds us that he was working to raise money for good causes right up to the very last months of his career in Evansville; the caption was "'U'—YOU Help to Bring It In!" A flaming torch represents the United Fund Campaign for 1958, and a figure representing the common man (although not Mr. Public) is seen walking through the U, from darkness to light, carrying

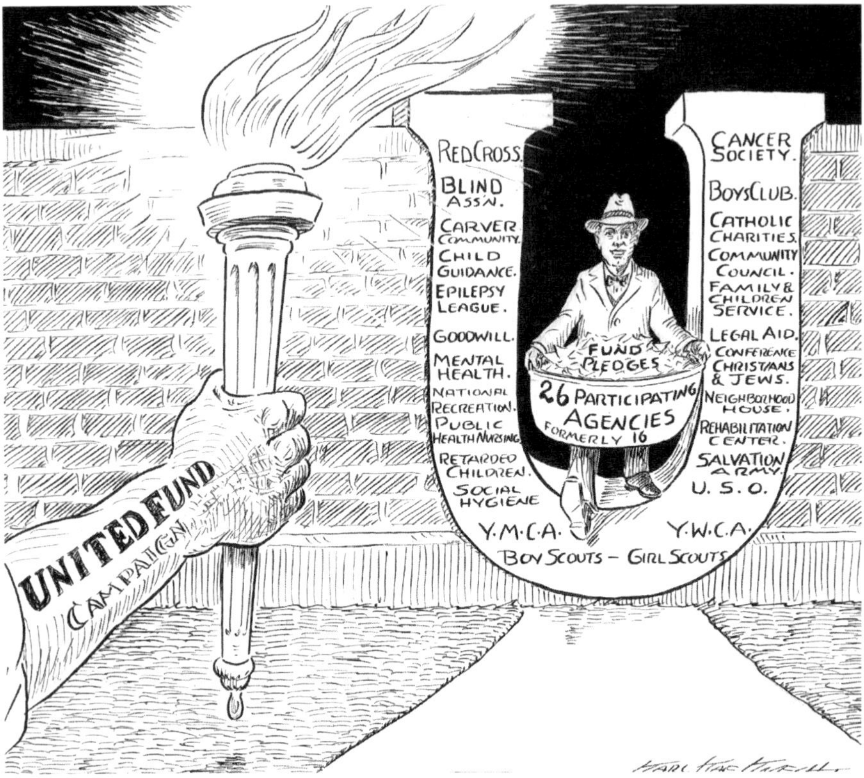

United Fund campaign, November 12, 1958. *UE/EVPL.*

pledges for the "26 participating agencies." Knecht then lists all twenty-six of the agencies prominently on the U. It is a superficially simple cartoon, but the subliminal message conveyed by the contrast of the light and the darkness is potent; it seems to be urging the viewer to come forward and help lighten the darkness with a pledge. The implicit message is that it will light the community but also perhaps bring light to your life. And it is reminiscent of many of his cartoons over the years in which the readers are addressed directly and given a clear role to play. A master communicator, Knecht used his skills always to try to improve the community that he had made his home, and this cartoon is a great example.

Conclusion

After battling illness for several years, Karl Kae Knecht died on July 28, 1972, at age eighty-eight. He was buried in Evansville's Oak Hill Cemetery.[217] The day after his funeral, the newspaper with which he was synonymous printed the following remarkable tribute on the front page that he himself had graced with his talents for forty-six years:

> *Karl Kae Knecht, cartoonist for* The Evansville Courier *for nearly 54 years, left a mark upon his time and the area in which he lived unique in the history of the Tri-state. His contributions to the growth and acceptance of this newspaper by its readers are incalculable. Words cannot express his varied interests, his keen insight into the future and its needs, that guided and shaped the artistry through which he spoke. The* Courier *believes its eulogy to Karl Kae Knecht best can be expressed by reprinting from the originals a variety of his cartoons published in this newspaper over the years. They appear this morning on the editorial page. Each of them speaks to us today just as they did when originally published and convey their message without the original captions, the professional test of fine cartoons. Rest in peace, Karl Kae Knecht.*[218]

It is, in its own way, an elegant and rather beautiful tribute; the key word, perhaps, is *unique*. Karl Kae Knecht was like nobody else. The city's other newspaper, the *Evansville Press*, published the following letter two weeks after his death: "There are many people that I respect, but none exceeds my admiration for K. K. Knecht, who treated me as a human being." It was signed "Ex-Office

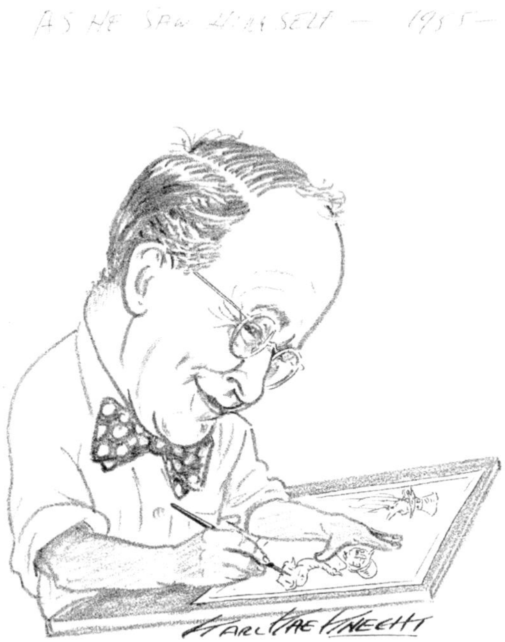

Karl Kae Knecht, self-portrait, 1955. *UE/EVPL.*

Boy of 50 Years Ago."[219] His old friend C.B. Enlow, chairman of the National City Bank, said on Knecht's retirement in 1960, "I cannot think of anyone I have ever known who has led a fuller life and contributed more to the every day enjoyment and inspiration of those privileged to see your daily cartoons in *The Evansville Courier*. There has been no one else like you….I recall so vividly the remembrance of your laughter, your joy and fun in living, and your never failing courage and optimism."[220]

A unique man who treated people as human beings, Karl Kae Knecht left his mark on Evansville, the country and, indeed, the world through his artistic activism. While guilty of peddling racist stereotypes at a time when almost everyone else was doing the same, ultimately what shines through his art over a lifetime of drawing is his humanity and his sense of humor. One former co-worker, Jim Palmer, said that his "unfailing kindness and good humor made life a good deal pleasanter for us all." His lifelong friend Marie Horton Woods said in 1960 that he was "solid and quiet and—I think the word is just good….[He is a] gracious and kindly gentleman….The office won't be quite the same without his quiet, cheery presence."[221] His cartoons were seldom loud, seldom ostentatious; in many ways, his activism spoke quietly. But speak it did, with great effectiveness, for over fifty-four years. When he left the *Courier*, his colleague Jeanne Suhrheinrich spoke of how "gloomy" it was to pass the now empty office of "one of the most vibrant personalities I've ever known."[222] The office was empty. The artist was gone. But the cartoons remain.

NOTES

INTRODUCTION

1. Hoff, *Editorial and Political Cartooning*, 13.
2. Greer, "Karl Knecht Remembered."
3. "Karl Kae Knecht," *Sunday Courier and Press*.
4. "Evansville Honors KKK," *Evansville Press*.
5. Dewey, *Art of Ill Will*; Hess and Kaplan, *Ungentlemanly Art*.
6. Quoted in Buck, "Defining the British Political Cartoon."
7. Rowson, *Giving Offence*, 39.
8. Navasky, *Art of Controversy*, xxi. Art can be, of course, a "weapon," see Philippe, *Political Graphics*.
9. "Renowned Courier Artist," *Evansville Courier*.
10. Mesner to Shaw, June 9, 1960. He was "known as the dean of American Political Cartoonists" ("Karl Kae Knecht," *Association of American Editorial Cartoonists News*, 1).
11. Ensley, *World of Karl Kae Knecht*, 4, 21; Pulitzer Prize Nomination Acknowledgement. Ensley incorrectly states that the nomination was in 1949.
12. "Century of Cartoons," *Evansville Courier and Press*; "Pen & Ink Politics," *Evansville Courier*; Giglio, *Truman in Cartoon and Caricature*. Knecht's cartoons also appear in analytical biographies of Presidents. See Maney, *Roosevelt Presence*, 160–61.
13. "Cartoonist Praised in Messages," *Evansville Courier*; Political Cartoon Society, *Low, the Twentieth Century's Greatest Cartoonist*; Laxman, "Freedom

to Cartoon," 74–75. The great Indian cartoonist R.K. Laxman has called Low "the greatest cartoonist the world had ever known."

14. "Real Pro Retires," *Evansville Courier*.
15. Lichtman, *Prejudice and the Old Politics*, 277–78. "Dry Democrats in the State at large bolted their ticket," and Smith did not even receive "the solid Catholic vote" in Indiana.
16. Bosse, *When Everybody Boosts Everybody Wins*.
17. Quoted in "150 Years of History," *Evansville Courier*.
18. "Karl Kae Knecht," *Sunday Courier and Press*.
19. Benedict to Scism, October 17, 1952.
20. "Correctly Delivered," *Evansville Courier*.
21. "Knecht Drawings Moved *Courier* Readers," *Evansville Courier*.
22. "Cartoonist Dean Visits Rochester," *Rochester Post-Bulletin*.
23. MacLeod, *Evansville in World War II*, 27.

CHAPTER 1

24. "Former Freeporter Was Honored Recently," *Freeport Journal*; "Distinguished Son Returns for Diamond Jubilee," *Iroquois Crier*; "Cartoonist Pays Homage to his Birthplace," *Evansville Courier*. Knecht drew a picture of the store in 1955.
25. "Menagerie Is Artist's Hobby," *Illinois Central Magazine*, 15; "First Cartoon of Karl Knecht," *Freeport Journal-Standard*. The cartoon showed W.T. Rawleigh, campaigning to be mayor of Freeport, atop an elephant, with the caption "Nothing Can Stop Him." Knecht was right—Rawleigh won.
26. "45 Years of Courier Cartoons," *Evansville Courier*.
27. "Karl Kae Knecht Today Begins 2nd Half-Century with *Courier*," *Evansville Courier*.
28. "Truly Amazing Production Record," *Indiana Business and Industry*, 14.
29. Howells and Matson, *Using Visual Evidence*, 33.
30. Carroll to Fehn, December 4, 1933.
31. Ensley, *World of Karl Kae Knecht*, 5; "45 Years of Courier Cartoons," *Evansville Courier*.
32. Marschall, "The Century in Political Cartoons," 54.
33. The twelve-page paper that day cost two cents, and the main headline on page 1 was "Taft Takes Over Government of Cuba." The weather forecast called for rain and cooler temperatures.
34. "Museum Will Exhibit Knecht Cartoons," *Evansville Courier*.

35. Hackleman, *Commercial Engraving and Printing*, 382; "One Score and Ten," *Evansville Courier*.
36. "Cartoonist Ki 'Professor' Now," *Evansville Courier*.
37. Knecht, "Chalk Plates."
38. Marschall, "Century in Political Cartoons," 55; "Improved 'Art,' Better News Pictures Help Make Courier Easier to Read," *Evansville Courier*.
39. Knecht, "These All on Chalk Plates." It actually says "crudness."
40. "Honors Heaped upon Knecht at Birthday Party," *Evansville Journal*.
41. "45 Years of Courier Cartoons," *Evansville Courier*.
42. *Karl Kae Knecht Hand-Drawn Notebooks*.
43. "Social and Personal," *Evansville Courier*.
44. Ensley, *World of Karl Kae Knecht*, 12.
45. Woods, "Knecht's Top Interest—His Wife," *Evansville Courier*.
46. "Jannie Knecht," *Sunday Courier and Press*.
47. "Speakers Allowed to Start, That's All," *Evansville Courier*.
48. "Lady Rotarians Refuse to Let K.K.K. See Dance," *Evansville Courier*.
49. "Knecht's Life Mirrors Twentieth Century History," *Evansville Courier*; "To Meet Truman," *Evansville Press*.
50. "Entertainment Given at Marine Hospital," *Evansville Courier*; "Boehne Camp Now Has Small Branch Library," ibid.; "Local Entertainers a Big Hit at West Baden," ibid; Engler, *Evansville*, 80. There is a photo of the U.S. Marine Hospital in Engler's book.
51. "K.K.K.'s Canes for West Baden Soldiers," *Evansville Courier*.
52. "Cane Shower Has Brought 200 Sticks," *Evansville Courier*; "K.K.K.'s Canes Christmas Gifts," ibid. "Alfred Bernardin sent two of his finest walking sticks." Bernardin was the founder of the Bernardin Bottle Cap Company.
53. "Thousands Visit Local USO Club," *Evansville Courier*.
54. "Cartoonist Will Give Lincoln USO Program," *Evansville Courier*. For race relations in Evansville, see Bigham, *We Ask Only a Fair Trial*.
55. "Visiting Committee Plans Camp Program," *Sunday Courier and Press*; "Special Party," *Facility Bulletin*; Newcomb to Knecht, October 11, 1944; Rowland to Knecht, November 4, 1944.
56. "Vaughn Shoemaker; Created John Q. Public," *New York Times*.
57. Piott, *Daily Life in the Progressive Era*, 118; Hess and Kaplan, *Ungentlemanly Art*, 34.
58. Dewey, *Art of Ill Will*, 20; Brookes, "Little Man and the Slump," 49. In Britain, there was Sidney Strube's "the Little Man," which appeared "every day on the editorial page." "This respectable bespectacled figure

with his bowler hat and umbrella was constantly shown at the mercy of the various 'vested interests' intent on wasting that part of his earnings which he paid in taxes." Laxman, "Freedom to Cartoon," 81–83. The Indian cartoonist R.K. Laxman also created a "ubiquitous…common man" after World War II--a Mr Indian Public—and he, too, was a "mute…bemused spectator of events which are beyond his control."

59. "'Dean of Cartoonists' Boosted Red Cross Spirit and Support," *Evansville Courier*.
60. Check to Knecht, June 6, 1960.
61. Ensley, *World of Karl Kae Knecht*, 57. Ensley mentions, among others, the "Association for the Blind, Big Sisters, Boy Scouts, Catholic Community Center, Family Welfare, Public Health Nursing Association, Red Cross, Rescue Mission, Salvation Army, Tuberculosis Association, Y.M.C.A., and Y.W.C.A…local hospitals, the March of Dimes, the Community Chest, and the United Fund."
62. Klinger, *We Face the Future Unafraid*, 28–33; Morlock, *Evansville Story*, 177.
63. Olmstead, *From Institute to University*, 25. University historian Ralph Olmstead famously said that attempting such a fundraising effort in 1917 was "at least folly, if not insanity."
64. Ensley, *World of Karl Kae Knecht*, 78–79.
65. Willard Library, Evansville Zoological Society and Mesker Park Zoo, *Pictorial History of Mesker Park Zoo*, 6.
66. "Lions Offered to City as 'Real' Zoo Nucleus," *Sunday Courier and Journal*.
67. "'King' and 'Queen' Are in New Home," *Evansville Journal*.
68. "Karl Kae Knecht," *Town and Country Review*.
69. "Start Fund to Buy Elephant for Zoo," *Sunday Courier and Press*.
70. "Whoopee! Elephant Fund Full," *Evansville Journal*. The family had in 1900 donated the land for the original Mesker Park; George L Mesker subsequently donated very large sums of money to improve the site.
71. "Mesker Zoo Story," *Evansville Courier*.
72. "At the Zoo," *Evansville Courier*.
73. "Zoo Attendant Taken by Death," *Evansville Press*.
74. "Zoo Superintendent Bob McGraw Dies," *Evansville Press*.
75. "Say Kay! Shows, N'Such by Karl Kae Knecht," *Sunday Courier and Press*. I am grateful to Erin Gibson for pointing this article out.
76. "Honors Heaped upon Knecht at Birthday Party," *Evansville Journal*.
77. Early to Fehn, December 4, 1933. It was signed by Stephen Early, who was FDR's press secretary.
78. Roosa to Fehn, December 4, 1933.

79. Noelting to Knecht, December 4, 1933; Eichel to Fehn, December 1, 1933.
80. Berndt et al. to Knecht, December 1933. The signers were Walter Berndt (who drew *Smitty*), Martin Branner (*Winnie Winkle*), Harold Gray (*Little Orphan Annie*), Frank King (*Gasoline Alley*), Carl Ed (*Harold Teen*), Frank Willard (*Moon Mullins*) and Sidney Smith (*The Gumps*).
81. "Honors Heaped upon Knecht at Birthday Party," *Evansville Journal*; Jensen, *Amazing Tom Mix*, 117.
82. McIntyre to Fehn, December 2, 1933.
83. Scism, "Real 'Guy,' in Other Words," *Evansville Courier Extra*.
84. "Folks Worth Knowing: Karl Kae Knecht," *Editor and Publisher*; "Cartoonists as They See Themselves: Karl Kae Knecht," *Literary Digest*, 10; "Karl Kae Knecht," *Town and Country Review*; Ensley, *World of Karl Kae Knecht*, 7–8.
85. McIntyre, "Mister Chairman, La-dees and Gents!" *Evansville Courier*.
86. Ensley, *World of Karl Kae Knecht*, 2.
87. "Karl Kae Knecht Today Begins 2nd Half-Century with Courier," *Evansville Courier*.
88. "Fifty Years of KKK," *Evansville Courier*.
89. "Creator of 18,000 Cartoons, *Courier*'s Karl Kae Retires," *Evansville Courier*.
90. Shaw, "Cartoonist's Impact on Area Great for Over Half Century," *Evansville Courier*.

Chapter 2

91. "Knecht in Chalk Talk," *Evansville Courier*, April 10, 1914; "Green Pastures," *Sunday Courier and Journal*.
92. McCutchan, Bartelt and Lonnberg, *Evansville at the Bend in the River*, 49.
93. "Housing Project to Start Monday," *Evansville Press*.
94. "Lincoln Gardens Improvement to the City," *Evansville Press*.
95. "Two Negroes Killed by Mob," *Evansville Courier*.
96. "Fatally Shoots Negro Over a Disputed Nickel," *Evansville Courier*.
97. Fischer, *Them Damned Pictures*, 72.
98. Lensmire and Snaza, "What Teacher Education Can Learn from Blackface Minstrelsy," 414.
99. Boskin, *Sambo*, 11.
100. Thibodeau, "From Racism to Tokenism," 492–93.
101. Fischer, *Them Damned Pictures*, 81.

102. Melton, *Sea Cobra*, 16–17; Cutler, *Battle of Leyte Gulf*, chapter 4.

103. "Broadway," *Evansville Courier*; United States Congress, *Congressional Record Proceedings and Debates of the…Congress*, A3783; "Rankin Hits US Coddling of Japs," *Evansville Press*.

104. "Halsey Fights Japs, but Dodges Female Reporters," *Evansville Press*.

105. Quoted in Dower, *War Without Mercy*, 78.

106. Sledge, *With the Old Breed at Peleliu and Okinawa*, 120; Weingartner, "Trophies of War," 56; Harrison, "Skull Trophies of the Pacific War," 817–20.

107. Johnson and Katz, *Herblock*, 93.

108. Minear, *Dr. Seuss Goes to War*, 25, 138–52.

109. Schiffrin, *Dr. Seuss & Co. Go to War*, 17–18.

110. Low and Howe, *Years of Wrath, A Cartoon History*; ibid., *Cartoon History of Our Times*; Bryant, *Illingworth's War in Cartoons*, 85.

111. Erenberg and Hirsch, *War in American Culture*, 237.

112. ShiPu Wang, "Japan Against Japan," 41. These images included the infamous "Tokio Kid Say" posters used by the Douglas Aircraft Company.

Chapter 3

113. Danjoux, "Reconsidering the Decline of the Editorial Cartoon," 246.

114. Klausen, *Cartoons That Shook the World*, 17.

115. Isquith, "'Enduring Power of Cartoons': How One Man's Response to Hebdo Went Viral." Evansville cartoonist James MacLeod said, "Cartoons, for some reason, have provoked this extreme reaction. Of all the things that these highly motivated, highly organized guys could have gone after, they went after a bunch of cartoonists. I think for me the attack illustrated once again the power of the cartoon, still, to have an enormous impact."

116. Bonilla, "Drawing Fire," 77; Abraham, "Anatomy of the Political Cartoon," 279. Abu Abraham said, "One of the tests of any free society is how free its cartoonists are."

117. "Ancient Origin of Cartoon Art Cited by Knecht," *Evansville Courier*.

118. Davis, "Political Cartoons Are Old Stuff," 382; Hoff, *Editorial and Political Cartooning*, 19–20.

119. Guiley, *Encyclopedia of Angels*, 216.

120. Klein, *Art and Laughter*, 13, 16.

121. Coupe, "Political and Religious Cartoons of the Thirty Years' War," 66.

122. Lindvall, *God Mocks*, 86–89; O'Hare, *Facts About Luther*, 158. Almost four hundred years later, the breathless Catholic apologist Father Patrick O'Hare could still say that these were "woodcuts [that] in obscenity and vulgarity have never been surpassed."

123. Philippe, *Political Graphics*, 54. Fascinatingly, this image is often mistakenly interpreted as an anti-Lutheran image. (Luther was, of course, also a monk.)

124. Heller and Anderson, *Savage Mirror*, 12.

125. Shesgreen, *Engravings by Hogarth*, xxiv.

126. Bryant and Heneage, *Dictionary of British Cartoonists and Caricaturists, 1730-1980*, 115.

127. "Hogarth, the Father of the Modern Cartoon," *Daily Telegraph*, November 1, 2014.

128. Hill, *Satirical Etchings of James Gillray*, ix.

129. Rowson, "Satire, Sewers and Statesmen."

130. Ibid., *Giving Offence*, 31–33.

131. Geipel, *Cartoon: A Short History of Graphic Comedy and Satire*, 64; Heard, *High Spirits*, 26. Rowlandson owned several of Hogarth's prints.

132. Phagan, Gatrell and Rauser, *Thomas Rowlandson*, 45, 11.

133. Geipel, *Cartoon: A Short History of Graphic Comedy and Satire*, 71; Bryant and Heneage, *Dictionary of British Cartoonists*, 51.

134. Vogler, *Graphic Works of George Cruikshank*, 135; Patten, *George Cruikshank's Life, Times, and Art*, 154–55.

135. Geipel, *Cartoon: A Short History of Graphic Comedy and Satire*, 71; Bryant and Heneage, *Dictionary of British Cartoonists*, 72, 74; Shikes and Heller, *The Art of Satire*, 17. The direct influence of English artists on French artists is seen, for example, in Eugene Delacroix's copying multiple prints by both Rowlandson and Gillray.

136. Kerr, *Caricature and French Political Culture*, 2.

137. Navasky, *Art of Controversy*, 71; Petrey, *In the Court of the Pear King*, 151. Sandy Petrey recently pointed out that "Louis-Philippe actually looked like a pear."

138. "Daumier: A Pauper in Life, a Master in Death," *Sunday Courier and Press*.

139. De la Motte and Przyblyski, *Making the News*, 55.

140. Vinson, *Thomas Nast*, 1.

141. "Speaker Here Tells History of Cartooning," *Evansville Press*.

142. Masters, "He Gave Politics the Donkey and Elephant," *Sunday Courier and Press*.

143. "Say Kay! What of Folks, Shows, Animals 'n' Such by Karl Kae Knecht," *Sunday Courier and Press*.

Chapter 4

144. I am grateful to Tom Lonnberg and Bill Bartelt for information conveyed at the opening to the exhibit *Lincoln's Boyhood in Indiana* at the Evansville Museum of Art, History and Science in 2016. The exhibit was sponsored by the Southwestern Indiana Historical Society.
145. "Knecht Speaks on Cartoons," *Evansville Courier.*
146. Kennedy, "Drawing (Cartoons) from Artistic Traditions," 10.
147. Bryant, *World's Greatest War Cartoonists and Caricaturists*, 133; Schwartz and Przyblyski, *Nineteenth-Century Visual Culture Reader*, 157–58. The image appears in Rappaport, *Shopping for Pleasure*, 163.
148. Knecht, "Chalk Plates."
149. For the accurate story of the founding of Evansville, see McCutchan, Bartelt and Lonnberg, *Evansville at the Bend in the River*, 10–12, and Morlock, *Evansville Story*, 13–17.
150. Bergfelder and Street, Titanic *in Myth and Memory*, 2.
151. Wachholz, *Eastland Disaster*, 7.
152. "Right in the Heart of a Great City," *Evansville Courier.*
153. Fallows, *Chicago's Awful Theater Horror*, 33; O'Donnell, *Ship Ablaze*; Renaud, *Into the Mist.*
154. United States Department of Labor, "U.S. Department of Labor—History."
155. Von Drehle, *Triangle*, 3.
156. "When Building Ordinances Are Not Enforced," *Evansville Courier.*
157. "It Should Be a Simple Matter to Find Those Who Are Really Responsible," *Evansville Courier.*
158. Examples include the cartoons for Memorial Day in 1929, 1942, 1947 and 1948.
159. Blatt, *Sons of Men.*
160. "James Montgomery Flagg," *Evansville Courier.*
161. "Throng Honors Soldier Hero," *Evansville Courier.*
162. "To Open Gresham Memorial Sunday," *Evansville Courier.*
163. "Plaza Shrine Proposed for Gresham," *Evansville Courier.*
164. "Bridge Open to Free Traffic Today as Celebration Starts," *Evansville Press*; "Public Views, Speakers Laud New Terminal," *Evansville Journal.*
165. Welky, *Thousand-Year Flood*, xi; Casto, *Great Ohio River Flood of 1937*, 7.
166. "When Disaster Strikes—Life Came to Halt as 1937 Flood Hit Region," *Evansville Courier and Press.*
167. McCutchan, Bartelt and Lonnberg, *Evansville at the Bend in the River*, 71.

168. "Thousands Watch Autogiro Flights," *Evansville Press*.
169. "Historical Sketch of the Courier and other Evansville Newspapers," *Evansville Courier*.
170. "New High Speed Printing Machine of the Latest Pattern is Another Milestone in Press Growth," *Evansville Press*.
171. Okrent, *Last Call*, ix.
172. Behr, *Prohibition*, 2.
173. Hoffman, *Scarface Al*, 24.
174. Blocker, Fahey, and Tyrrell, *Alcohol and Temperance in Modern History*, 440.
175. McNeese, *Great Depression*, 64.
176. McElvaine, *Great Depression*, 160.
177. Ward, Brough and Arnold, *Historical Dictionary*, 147.
178. Wilson, *U.S. Justice System*, 946.

Chapter 5

179. Zeiler, *Annihilation*, 412.
180. *What America Thinks*, 92, 150, 246, 712, 718. He was, of course, well aware of the gathering war clouds long before Pearl Harbor—five of his cartoons are included in a collection of American editorials and cartoons published in 1941, featuring cartoons from 1938 to 1941.
181. Zeman, *Heckling Hitler*, 98–99.
182. Benson, *Illingworth*, 51. In an interesting mirror to Knecht's cartoon, this moment was memorably represented by the British cartoonist Leslie Illingworth on June 23, 1941, as Hitler stabbing Stalin in the back while in the act of hugging him.
183. Herf, *Jewish Enemy*, 252. According to Jeffrey Herf, "Even in the months following D-day, about 68.5 percent of all German battlefield deaths occurred on the eastern front."
184. James, *Picture This*, 69.
185. Clark, "'You Are Here,'" 578.
186. Roeder, *Censored War*, 13–14;
187. Dower, *Cultures of War*, 214.
188. "Three Americans," *Life*.
189. Brookes, "'Everything in the Garden is Lovely,'" 35; Douglas, *World War*, 247. It is worth noting that Sidney Strube, "arguably Britain's most widely known cartoonist," drew a cartoon in the *Daily Express* on April 30, 1945, showing *Mein Kampf* being crushed by an Allied boot.

190. Yoe, *Great Anti-War Cartoons*, 116.
191. "One Hope," *Evansville Courier*.
192. Jansohn, *President Truman and (the Challenge of) the Potsdam Conference 1945*, 1.
193. Wathen, "Evansville Needs Grand Reminder of Its Efforts During War," *Evansville Courier*; see also Bigham, *Evansville*; Kellar and Kellar, *Evansville Shipyard*; Gourley, *Shipyard Work Force*; Morgan, *Home Front Heroes*; and Morgan, *Home Front Warriors*.
194. All these letters are in the University of Evansville Archives.
195. Igleheart to Knecht, June 8, 1944; "Local Women Producing Supplies for Hospitals," *Evansville Courier*. As early as November 1942, Mrs Igleheart had been calling for hundreds of extra volunteers. See also Harris, "Rolling Bandages and Building Thunderbolts."
196. Schaeffer to Knecht, May 23, 1945.
197. His invitation and platform ticket stub are both in the University of Evansville Archives.
198. MacLeod, *Evansville in World War II*, 41; *LST 325*.
199. For Indiana's war effort, see Max Cavnes's magisterial work: Cavnes, *Hoosier Community at War*.
200. MacLeod, *Evansville in World War II*, 70; Gabin, "Women Defense Workers in World War II," 109, 117.
201. McWhirter to Harrison, June 1942.
202. Karsten, *Encyclopedia of War & American Society*, 668. "Slogans such as 'Loose Lips Sink Ships' became part of everyday language" during the war.
203. Buell, and Maus, "Is the Pen Mightier Than the Word?," 847. "As long as editorial cartoonists have caricatured politicians, politicians have feared for their public images."

Chapter 6

204. Ensley, *The World of Karl Kae Knecht*, 25.
205. Bigham, *We Ask Only a Fair Trial*; Madison, *Lynching in the Heartland*.
206. Martin, *Indiana, an Interpretation*, 184; Moore, *Citizen Klansmen*, 14; Tucker, *Notre Dame vs. the Klan*, 73–74. For a brilliant summary of the Klan in Indiana in the 1920s, see Madison, *Hoosiers*, 242–53.
207. "Ku Klux Klan, Flaunting 'White Supremacy' Banner, Reborn in Georgia Ceremony," *Evansville Press*.
208. Ryan and Schlup, *Historical Dictionary of the 1940s*, 370.

209. Conlin, *American Past*, 725.
210. Morris, *1948*, 180–97.
211. Drawn on December 4, 1947.
212. "Reds Sweep Within 70 Miles of Pusan," *Evansville Courier*.
213. "Truman Advisors Favor Building Hydrogen Bomb," *Evansville Courier*; "Speed on H-Bomb Asked by Truman," ibid. Truman would make the announcement that the hydrogen bomb would indeed get built on January 31.
214. "World Eyes Moscow," *Evansville Courier*.
215. "Local GOP Ready for Nixon Visit," *Evansville Courier*.
216. "Second Thoughts," *Evansville Courier*.

Conclusion

217. "Knecht Services Set for Today," *Evansville Courier*.
218. "Cartoons by Knecht Express our Eulogy," *Evansville Courier*.
219. "Around Town," *Evansville Press*.
220. Enlow to Knecht, May 31, 1960.
221. Palmer to Knecht, June 4, 1960; "From My Tower," *Evansville Courier*.
222. "Front Row Center," *Evansville Courier*.

BIBLIOGRAPHY

Abraham, Abu. "Anatomy of the Political Cartoon." *India International Centre Quarterly* 2, no. 4 (October 1975): 273–79.

Bal, Anjali S., Leyland Pitt, Pierre Berthon and Philip DesAutels. "Caricatures, Cartoons, Spoofs and Satires: Political Brands as Butts." *Journal of Public Affairs* 9, no. 4 (2009): 229–37.

Behr, Edward. *Prohibition: Thirteen Years That Changed America*. New York: Arcade Publishing, 1996.

Benedict, G.R., to Don Scism, October 17, 1952. University of Evansville Archives.

Benson, Tim. "The Greatest Political Cartoon of All Time?" *History Today* 55, no. 3 (March 2005), 20–23.

Benson, Timothy S. *Illingworth: Political Cartoons from the Daily Mail 1939–69*. London: Political Cartoon Society, 2009.

Bergfelder, Tim, and Sarah Street. *The* Titanic *in Myth and Memory: Representations in Visual and Literary Culture*. London: I.B. Tauris, 2004.

Berndt, Walter, et al. to Karl Kae Knecht, December 8, 1933. University of Evansville Archives.

Bigham, Darrel E. *Evansville: The World War II Years*. Charleston, SC: Arcadia Publishing, 2005.

———. *We Ask Only a Fair Trial: A History of the Black Community of Evansville, Indiana*. Bloomington: Indiana University Press, 1987.

Bigi, Alessandro, Kirk Plangger, Michelle Bonera and Colin L. Campbell. "When Satire Is Serious: How Political Cartoons Impact a Country's Brand." *Journal of Public Affairs* 11, no. 3 (2011): 148–55.

Blatt, Heiman Kimmel. *Sons of Men; Evansville's War Record.* Evansville, IN: Abe P. Madison, 1920.

Blocker, Jack S., David M. Fahey and Ian R. Tyrrell. *Alcohol and Temperance in Modern History: An International Encyclopedia.* Vol. 1. Santa Barbara, CA: ABC-CLIO, 2003.

Bonilla, Xavier. "Drawing Fire: South American Cartoonists' Battle with Censorship." *Index on Censorship* 43, no. 4 (December 2014): 77–80.

Boskin, Joseph. *Sambo: The Rise & Demise of an American Jester.* New York: Oxford University Press, 1986.

Bosse, Jeffrey A. *When Everybody Boosts Everybody Wins: The Untold Story of Evansville Mayor Benjamin Bosse.* Evansville, IN: M.T. Publishing Company, 2014.

Brookes, Rod. "'Everything in the Garden Is Lovely': The Representation of National Identity in Sidney Strube's Daily Express Cartoons in the 1930s." *Oxford Art Journal* 13, no. 2 (1990): 31–43.

———. "The Little Man and the Slump: Sidney Strube's Cartoons and the Politics of Unemployment 1929–1931." *Oxford Art Journal* 8, no. 1 (1985): 49–61.

Bryant, Mark. *Illingworth's War in Cartoons: One Hundred of His Greatest Drawings from the* Daily Mail, *1939–1945.* London: Grub Street, 2009.

———. *The World's Greatest War Cartoonists and Caricaturists, 1792–1945.* London: Grub Street, 2011.

Bryant, Mark, and Simon Heneage. *Dictionary of British Cartoonists and Caricaturists, 1730–1980.* Aldershot, Hants, UK: Scolar Press, 1994.

Buck, Louisa. "Defining the British Political Cartoon." Inter-Disciplinary.Ne: A Global Network for Dynamic Research and Publishing. http://www.inter-disciplinary.net/at-the-interface/wp-content/uploads/2013/07/LBuck-wpaper-gn2.pdf.

Buell, Emmett H., Jr., and Mike Maus. "Is the Pen Mightier Than the Word? Editorial Cartoons and 1988 Presidential Nominating Politics." *PS: Political Science and Politics* 21, no. 4 (Fall 1988): 847–58.

Carroll, Percy, to Ed Fehn, December 4, 1933. University of Evansville Archives.

"Cartoonists as They See Themselves: Karl Kae Knecht." *Literary Digest* 118, no. 2 (July 1934): 10.

Casto, James E. *The Great Ohio River Flood of 1937.* Charleston, SC: Arcadia Publishing, 2009.

Cavnes, Max. *The Hoosier Community at War.* Bloomington: Indiana University Press, 1961.

Check, Francis, to Karl Kae Knecht, June 6, 1960. University of Evansville Archives.

Clark, Constance A. "'You Are Here': Missing Links, Chains of Being, and the Language of Cartoons." *Isis* 100, no. 3 (September 2009): 571–89.

Conlin, Joseph Robert. *The American Past. A Survey of American History*. Vol. 2. Princeton, NJ: Cengage Learning, 2006.

Conners, Joan L. "Popular Culture in Political Cartoons: Analyzing Cartoonist Approaches." *PS: Political Science & Politics* 40, no. 2 (2007): 261–65.

Coupe, W.A. "Political and Religious Cartoons of the Thirty Years' War." *Journal of the Warburg and Courtauld Institutes* 25, nos. 1–2 (January 1962): 65–86.

Cutler, Thomas J. *The Battle of Leyte Gulf, 23–26 October, 1944*. New York: HarperCollins, 1994.

Daily Telegraph. "Hogarth, the Father of the Modern Cartoon." November 1, 2014.

Danjoux, Ilan. "Reconsidering the Decline of the Editorial Cartoon." *PS: Political Science & Politics* 40, no. 2 (April 2007): 245–48.

Davis, Emily C. "Political Cartoons Are Old Stuff." *Science Newsletter* 29, no. 792 (June 1936): 382–84.

De la Motte, Dean, and Jeannene M. Przyblyski. *Making the News: Modernity & the Mass Press in Nineteenth-Century France*. Boston: University of Massachusetts Press, 1999.

Dewey, Donald. *The Art of Ill Will: The Story of American Political Cartoons*. New York: New York University Press, 2007.

Douglas, Roy. *The World War, 1939–1945: The Cartoonist's Vision*. London: Routledge, 1990.

Dower, John W. *Cultures of War: Pearl Harbor, Hiroshima, 9-11, Iraq*. New York: W.W. Norton, 2010.

———. *War Without Mercy: Race and Power in the Pacific War*. New York: Pantheon Books, 1986.

Early, Stephen, to Ed Fehn, December 4, 1933. University of Evansville Archives.

Editor and Publisher. "Folks Worth Knowing: Karl Kae Knecht." August 1935.

Eichel, Leslie, to Ed Fehn, December 1, 1933. University of Evansville Archives.

Engler, Joseph. *Evansville*. Charleston, SC: Arcadia Publishing, 2012.

Enlow, C.B., to Karl Kae Knecht, May 31, 1960. University of Evansville Archives.

Ensley, Philip C. *The World of Karl Kae Knecht Through His Cartoons*. Evansville, IN: University of Evansville Press, 1979.

Erenberg, Lewis A., and Susan E. Hirsch. *The War in American Culture: Society and Consciousness During World War II*. Chicago: University of Chicago Press, 1996.

Evansville Courier. "Ancient Origin of Cartoon Art Cited by Knecht." January 22, 1940.

———. "At the Zoo." June 22, 1990.

———. "Boehne Camp Now Has Small Branch Library." April 10, 1919.
———. "Broadway." October 16, 1943.
———. "Cane Shower Has Brought 200 Sticks." October 16, 1918.
———. "Cartoonist Ki 'Professor' Now." December 11, 1913.
———. "Cartoonist Praised in Messages from Personages from All Over the World." July 21, 1954.
———. "Cartoonist Will Give Lincoln USO Program." September 16, 1944.
———. "Cartoons by Knecht Express Our Eulogy." August 1, 1972.
———. "Correctly Delivered." March 3, 1937.
———. "Creator of 18,000 Cartoons, *Courier*'s Karl Kae Retires." June 1, 1960.
———. "'Dean of Cartoonists' Boosted Red Cross Spirit and Support." March 22, 1992.
———. "Entertainment Given at Marine Hospital." November 26, 1919.
———. "Fatally Shoots Negro over a Disputed Nickel." December 1, 1901.
———. "Fifty Years of KKK." September 27, 1956.
———. "45 Years of *Courier* Cartoons." September 12, 1951.
———. "From My Tower." June 3, 1960.
———. "Front Row Center." June 6, 1960.
———. "Historical Sketch of the *Courier* and other Evansville Newspapers." March 27, 1910.
———. "Improved 'Art,' Better News Pictures Help Make *Courier* Easier to Read." January 7, 1970.
———. "It Should Be a Simple Matter to Find Those Who Are Really Responsible." November 16, 1928.
———. "James Montgomery Flagg." May 31, 1960.
———. "K.K.K.'s Canes Christmas Gifts." December 26, 1918.
———. "K.K.K.'s Canes for West Baden Soldiers." December 15, 1918.
———. "Karl Kae Knecht Today Begins 2nd Half-Century with *Courier*." September 27, 1956.
———. "Knecht Drawings Moved *Courier* Readers." August 9, 1995.
———. "Knecht in Chalk Talk." April 10, 1914.
———. "Knecht Services Set for Today." July 31, 1972.
———. "Knecht's Life Mirrors Twentieth Century History." July 21, 1954.
———. "Knecht Speaks on Cartoons." October 9, 1947.
———. "Lady Rotarians Refuse to Let K.K.K. See Dance." February 1, 1918.
———. "Local Entertainers a Big Hit at West Baden." February 9, 1919.
———. "Local GOP Ready for Nixon Visit." October 15, 1956.
———. "Local Women Producing Supplies for Hospitals." November 6, 1942.
———. "Museum Will Exhibit Knecht Cartoons." August 19, 1985.
———. "Nixon, Lodge Offer Maturity, Experience." September 30, 1960.

———. "One Hope." August 11, 1945.

———. "150 Years of History Knecht's 54 Years with *Courier* Believed Cartooning Record." August 8, 1995.

———. "One Score and Ten." October 1, 1936.

———. "Pen & Ink Politics. Knecht Cartoons Featured in Shows at Evansville Museum and Truman Library." August 30, 1996.

———. "Plaza Shrine Proposed for Gresham." November 26, 1936.

———. "A Real Pro Retires." June 2, 1960.

———. "Reds Sweep Within 70 Miles of Pusan." July 26, 1950.

———. "Renowned *Courier* Artist, Cartoonist Emeritus, Karl Kae Knecht, Dies." July 29, 1972.

———. "Right in the Heart of a Great City." July 25, 1915.

———. "Second Thoughts." November 6, 1957.

———. "Social and Personal." August 22, 1918.

———. "Speakers Allowed to Start, That's All." February 25, 1919.

———. "Speed on H-Bomb Asked by Truman." February 1, 1950.

———. "The Cartoonist Pays Homage to His Birthplace." July 11, 1955.

———. "The Mesker Zoo Story." August 21, 1978.

———. "The World Eyes Moscow." March 5, 1953.

———. "Thousands Visit Local USO Club." November 23, 1943.

———. "Throng Honors Soldier Hero." November 12, 1917.

———. "To Open Gresham Memorial Sunday." August 13, 1918.

———. "Truman Advisors Favor Building Hydrogen Bomb." January 20, 1950.

———. "Two Negroes Killed by Mob." October 7, 1906.

———. "When Building Ordinances Are Not Enforced." March 27, 1911.

Evansville Courier and Press. "A Century of Cartoons." February 22, 2007.

———. "When Disaster Strikes—Life Came to Halt as 1937 Flood Hit Region." January 7, 2007.

Evansville Journal. "Honors Heaped upon Knecht at Birthday Party." December 5, 1933.

———. "'King" and "Queen" Are in New Home." April 23, 1928.

———. "Public Views, Speakers Laud New Terminal." February 27, 1931.

———. "Whoopee! Elephant Fund Full." April 10, 1929.

Evansville Press. "Around Town." August 9, 1972.

———. "Bridge Open to Free Traffic Today as Celebration Starts." July 3, 1932.

———. "Evansville Honors KKK. 500 Persons Pay Tribute to 'Dean' of Cartoonists at Noon Luncheon." July 21, 1954.

———. "Halsey Fights Japs, but Dodges Female Reporters." February 20, 1945.

———. "Housing Project to Start Monday." January 12, 1936.

———. "Ku Klux Klan, Flaunting 'White Supremacy' Banner, Reborn in Georgia Ceremony." May 10, 1946.

———. "Lincoln Gardens Improvement to the City. New Negro Housing Plan Replaces Slums." July 10, 1938.

———. "New High Speed Printing Machine of the Latest Pattern Is Another Milestone in Press Growth." July 29, 1921.

———. "Nixon Concedes After Kennedy Clinches Victory in California." November 9, 1960.

———. "Rankin Hits US Coddling of Japs." February 4, 1943.

———. "Speaker Here Tells History of Cartooning." January 22, 1940.

———. "Thousands Watch Autogiro Flights." September 21, 1931.

———. "To Meet Truman." October 3, 1949.

———. "Zoo Attendant Taken by Death." September 24, 1936.

———. "Zoo Superintendent Bob McGraw Dies." February 2, 1954.

Facility Bulletin (Veterans Administration, Danville, IL). "Special Party." October 27, 1944.

Fallows, Samuel. *Chicago's Awful Theater Horror, by the Survivors and Rescuers*. Chicago: Memorial Pub. Co, 1904.

Fischer, Roger A. *Them Damned Pictures: Explorations in American Political Cartoon Art*. North Haven, CT: Archon Books, 1996.

Freeport Journal. "A Former Freeporter Was Honored Recently." August 19, 1955.

Freeport Journal-Standard. "The First Cartoon of Karl Knecht." April 1, 1955.

Gabin, Nancy Felice. "Women Defense Workers in World War II: Views of Gender Equality in Indiana." In *The Home-Front War: World War II and American Society*, edited by Kenneth Paul O'Brien and Lynn H. Parsons, 107–18. Westport, CT: Greenwood Press, 1995.

Geipel, John. *The Cartoon: A Short History of Graphic Comedy and Satire*. New York: A.S. Barnes, 1972.

Giglio, James N. *Truman in Cartoon and Caricature*. Kirksville, MO: Truman State University Press, 2001.

Goodwin, George M. "More Than a Laughing Matter: Cartoons and Jews." *Modern Judaism* 21, no. 2 (May 2001): 146–74.

Gourley, Harold E. *Shipyard Work Force: World's Champion LST Builders on the Beautiful Ohio, 1942–1945, Evansville, IN*. Evansville, IN: LST Work Force, 1996.

Greer, Bill. "Karl Knecht Remembered." *Sunday Courier and Press*, July 30, 1972.

Guiley, Rosemary. *Encyclopedia of Angels*. New York: Facts on File, 1996.

Guyer, Jonathan. "The Offending Art. Political Cartooning After the *Charlie Hebdo* Attacks." *Nieman Reports*, Winter 2015: 33–41.

Hackleman, Charles W. *Commercial Engraving and Printing*. Indianapolis, IN: Commercial Engraving Publishing Company, 1921.

Harris, James R. "Rolling Bandages and Building Thunderbolts: A Woman's Memories of the Kentucky Home Front, 1941–45." *Register of the Kentucky Historical Society* 100, no. 2 (Spring 2002): 167–94.

Harrison, Simon. "Skull Trophies of the Pacific War: Transgressive Objects of Remembrance." *Journal of the Royal Anthropological Institute* 12, no. 4 (2006): 817–36.

Heard, Kate. *High Spirits: The Comic Art of Thomas Rowlandson*. London: Royal Collection Trust, 2013.

Heller, Steven, and Gail Anderson. *The Savage Mirror: The Art of Contemporary Caricature*. New York: Watson-Guptill, 1992.

Herf, Jeffrey. *Jewish Enemy Nazi Propaganda During World War II and the Holocaust*. Cambridge, MA: Harvard University Press, 2009.

Hess, Stephen, and Milton Kaplan. *The Ungentlemanly Art: A History of American Political Cartoons*. New York: Macmillan, 1975.

Hill, Draper, ed. *The Satirical Etchings of James Gillray*. New York: Dover Publications, 1976.

Hoff, Syd. *Editorial and Political Cartooning: From Earliest Times to the Present, with Over 700 Examples from the Works of the World's Greatest Cartoonists*. New York: Stravon Educational Press, 1976.

Hoffman, Dennis Earl. *Scarface Al and the Crime Crusaders Chicago's Private War Against Capone*. Carbondale: Southern Illinois University Press, 2010.

Howells, Richard, and Robert W. Matson, eds. *Using Visual Evidence*. Milton Keynes: Open University Press, 2009.

Husband, Tony. *Cartoons of World War II*. London: Arcturus, 2013.

Igleheart, Aline, to Karl Kae Knecht, June 8, 1944. University of Evansville Archives.

Iroquois Crier (South Dakota). "Distinguished Son Returns for Diamond Jubilee." June 23, 1955.

Isquith, Elias. "'Enduring Power of Cartoons': How One Man's Response to *Hebdo* Went Viral." Salon. http://www.salon.com/2015/01/21/enduring_power_of_cartoons_how_one_mans_response_to_hebdo_went_viral.

James, Pearl, ed. *Picture This: World War I Posters and Visual Culture*. Lincoln: University of Nebraska Press, 2009.

Jansohn, Uwe F. *President Truman and (the Challenge of) the Potsdam Conference 1945*. N.p.: Pickle Partners Publishing, 2013.

Jensen, Richard D. *The Amazing Tom Mix: The Most Famous Cowboy of the Movies*. New York: iUniverse, 2005.

Johnson, Haynes, and Harry L. Katz. *Herblock: The Life and Work of the Great Political Cartoonist*. Washington, D.C.: Herb Block Foundation, 2009.

"Karl Kae Knecht, Cartoonist Dean, Is Now 'Emeritus.'" *Association of American Editorial Cartoonists News*, June 1960.

Karl Kae Knecht Hand-Drawn Notebooks. 2 vols. University of Southern Indiana Archives, 1909.

"Karl Kae Knecht. Outstanding American Cartoonist." *Town and Country Review [London]* 6, no. 1 (November 1934): 1–2.

Karsten, Peter. *Encyclopedia of War & American Society*. Thousand Oaks, CA: Sage Publications, 2005.

Kellar, James H., and Patricia C. Kellar. *The Evansville Shipyard: Outside Any Shipbuilding Zone*. Bloomington, IN: Round Hill Press, 1999.

Kemnitz, Thomas M. "The Cartoon as a Historical Source." *Journal of Interdisciplinary History* 4, no. 1 (Summer 1973): 81–93.

Kennedy, Martha H. "Drawing (Cartoons) from Artistic Traditions." *American Art* 22, no. 1 (Spring 2008): 10–15.

Kerr, David S. *Caricature and French Political Culture, 1830–1848: Charles Philipon and the Illustrated Press*. Oxford, UK: Clarendon Press, 2000.

Klausen, Jytte. *The Cartoons That Shook the World*. New Haven, CT: Yale University Press, 2009.

Klein, Sheri. *Art and Laughter*. London: I.B. Taurus, 2007.

Klinger, George. *We Face the Future Unafraid: A Narrative History of the University of Evansville*. Evansville, IN: University of Evansville Press, 2003.

Knecht, Karl K. "Chalk Plates." University of Evansville Archives.

———. "These All on Chalk Plates." University of Evansville Archives.

"Knecht of the Evansville Courier." *Cartoons Magazine* 3, no. 4 (April 1913): 15–16.

Lamb, Chris. *Drawn to Extremes: The Use and Abuse of Editorial Cartoons*. New York: Columbia University Press, 2004.

Laxman, R.K. "Freedom to Cartoon, Freedom to Speak." *Daedalus* 118, no. 4 (Fall 1989): 68–91.

Lensmire, T.J., and N. Snaza. "What Teacher Education Can Learn from Blackface Minstrelsy." *Educational Researcher* 39, no. 5 (2010): 413–22.

Lewis, Helen. "Ink-Stained Assassins." *New Statesman* 141, no. 5120 (August 2012): 20–27.

Lichtman, Allan J. *Prejudice and the Old Politics: The Presidential Election of 1928*. Chapel Hill: University of North Carolina Press, 1979.

Lindvall, Terry. *God Mocks: A History of Religious Satire from the Hebrew Prophets to Stephen Colbert*. New York: NYU Press, 2015.

Low, David, and Quincy Howe. *A Cartoon History of Our Times*. New York: Simon and Schuster, 1939.

———. *Years of Wrath, A Cartoon History: 1931–1945*. New York: Simon and Schuster, 1946.

LST 325: Workhorse of the Waves & Evansville's War Machine, 1942–45. Evansville, IN: Evansville Courier & Press, 2005.

MacLeod, James Lachlan. *Evansville in World War II*. Charleston, SC: The History Press, 2015.

Madison, James H. *Hoosiers: A New History of Indiana*. Bloomington: Indiana University Press, 2014.

———. *A Lynching in the Heartland: Race and Memory in America*. New York: Palgrave, 2003.

Maney, Patrick J. *The Roosevelt Presence: The Life and Legacy of FDR*. Berkeley: University of California Press, 1998.

Marschall, Richard E. "The Century in Political Cartoons." *Columbia Journalism Review* 38, no. 1 (May/June 1999): 54–65.

Martin, John Bartlow. *Indiana, an Interpretation*. New York: A.A. Knopf, 1947.

Masters, Mildred. "He Gave Politics the Donkey and Elephant." *Sunday Courier and Press*, September 22, 1940.

McCutchan, Kenneth P., William E. Bartelt and Thomas R. Lonnberg. *Evansville at the Bend in the River: An Illustrated History*. Sun Valley, CA: American Historical Press, 2004.

McElvaine, Robert S. *The Great Depression: America, 1929–1941*. New York: Times Books, 1984.

McIntyre, O.O., to Ed Fehn, December 2, 1933. University of Evansville Archives.

McIntyre, O.O. "Mister Chairman, La-dees and Gents!" *Evansville Courier*, November 22, 1936.

McNeese, Tim. *The Great Depression, 1929–1938*. New York: Chelsea House, 2010.

McWhirter, F.W., to Frank Harrison, June 1942. Evansville Museum Archives.

Melton, Buckner F. *Sea Cobra: Admiral Halsey's Task Force and the Great Pacific Typhoon*. Guilford, CT: Lyons Press, 2007.

"Menagerie Is Artist's Hobby." *Illinois Central Magazine*, December 1930.

Mesner, Elmer, to Earl Shaw, June 9, 1960. University of Evansville Archives.

Minear, Richard H. *Dr. Seuss Goes to War: The World War II Editorial Cartoons of Theodor Seuss Geisel*. London: I.B. Tauris, 2004.

Moore, Leonard J. *Citizen Klansmen. The Ku Klux Klan in Indiana, 1921–1928*. Chapel Hill: University of North Carolina Press, 1991.

Moreno, Richard. *It Happened in Illinois: Remarkable Events That Shaped History*. Guilford, CT: Globe Pequot Press, 2011.

Morgan, Harold B. *Home Front Heroes: Evansville and the Tri-State in WWII*. Evansville, IN: M.T. Publishing Co, 2007.

———. *Home Front Warriors: Building the P-47 Thunderbolt and the LST Warship in Evansville, Indiana During World War II*. Evansville, IN: Harold B. Morgan, 2011.

Morlock, James E. *The Evansville Story. A Cultural Interpretation*. Evansville, IN: Creative Press, 1956.

Morris, Benny. *1948: A History of the First Arab-Israeli War*. New Haven, CT: Yale University Press, 2008.

Moss, Dori. "The Animated Persuader." *PS: Political Science & Politics* 40, no. 2 (April 2007): 241–44.

Navasky, Victor S. *The Art of Controversy: Political Cartoons and Their Enduring Power*. New York: Alfred A. Knopf, 2013.

Newcomb, Richard, to Karl Kae Knecht, October 11, 1944. University of Evansville Archives.

New York Times. "Vaughn Shoemaker; Created John Q. Public." August 22, 1991.

Noelting, Elmer, to Karl Kae Knecht, December 4, 1933. University of Evansville Archives.

O'Brien, Kenneth Paul, and Lynn H. Parsons. *The Home-Front War: World War II and American Society*. Westport, CT: Greenwood Press, 1995.

O'Donnell, Edward T. *Ship Ablaze: The Tragedy of the Steamboat General Slocum*. New York: Broadway Books, 2003.

O'Hare, Patrick F. *The Facts About Luther*. New York: F. Pustet & Co., 1916.

Okrent, Daniel. *Last Call: The Rise and Fall of Prohibition*. New York: Simon and Schuster, 2010.

Olmstead, Ralph. *From Institute to University: Moores Hill Male and Female Collegiate Institute*. Evansville, IN: University of Evansville Press, 1973.

Palmer, Jim, to Karl Kae Knecht, June 4, 1960. University of Evansville Archives.

Patten, Robert L. *George Cruikshank's Life, Times, and Art*. New Brunswick, NJ: Rutgers University Press, 1992.

Petrey, Sandy. *In the Court of the Pear King: French Culture and the Rise of Realism*. Ithaca, NY: Cornell University Press, 2005.

Phagan, Patricia, Vic Gatrell and Amelia F. Rauser. *Thomas Rowlandson: Pleasures and Pursuits in Georgian England*. Poughkeepsie, NY: Frances Lehman Loeb Art Center, Vassar College, 2011.

Philippe, Robert. *Political Graphics: Art as a Weapon*. New York: Abbeville Press, 1982.

Piott, Steven L. *Daily Life in the Progressive Era*. Santa Barbara, CA: Greenwood, 2011.

Political Cartoon Society. *Low, the Twentieth Century's Greatest Cartoonist*. London: BBC History Magazine, 2002.

Pulitzer Prize Nomination Acknowledgement, 1944. University of Evansville Archives.

Rajski, Raymond B. *A Nation Grieved: The Kennedy Assassination in Editorial Cartoons*. Rutland, VT: C.E. Tuttle Co, 1967.

Ramsey, E.M. "Inventing Citizens During World War I: Suffrage Cartoons in the Woman Citizen." *Western Journal of Communication* 64, no. 2 (2000): 113–47.

Rappaport, Erika Diane. *Shopping for Pleasure: Women in the Making of London's West End*. Princeton, NJ: Princeton University Press, 2000.

Renaud, Anne. *Into the Mist: The Story of the Empress of Ireland*. Toronto: Dundurn Press, 2010.

Rochester (Minnesota) Post-Bulletin. "Cartoonist Dean Visits Rochester." July 21, 1955.

Roeder, George H. *The Censored War: American Visual Experience During World War Two*. New Haven, CT: Yale University Press, 1993.

Roosa, Howard, to Ed Fehn, December 4, 1933. University of Evansville Archives.

Rowland, George, to Karl Kae Knecht, November 4, 1944. University of Evansville Archives.

Rowson, Martin. *Giving Offence*. London: Seagull Books, 2009.

———. "Satire, Sewers and Statesmen: Why James Gillray Was King of the Cartoon." *The Guardian* (London), March 21, 2015.

Ryan, James Gilbert, and Leonard C. Schlup. *Historical Dictionary of the 1940s*. Armonk, NY: M.E. Sharpe, 2006.

Schaeffer, Michael, to Karl Kae Knecht, May 23, 1945. University of Evansville Archives.

Schiffrin, André. *Dr. Seuss & Co. Go to War: The World War II Editorial Cartoons of America's Leading Comic Artists*. New York: New Press, 2009.

Schwartz, Vanessa R., and Jeannene M. Przyblyski. *The Nineteenth-Century Visual Culture Reader*. New York: Routledge, 2004.

Scism, Don. "A Real 'Guy,' in Other Words." *Evansville Courier Extra*, December 4, 1933.

Shaw, Earl E. "Cartoonist's Impact on Area Great for Over Half Century." *Evansville Courier*, June 3, 1960.

Shesgreen, Sean, ed. *Engravings by Hogarth: 101 Prints*. New York: Dover Publications, 1973.

Shikes, Ralph E., and Steven Heller. *The Art of Satire: Painters as Caricaturists and Cartoonists from Delacroix to Picasso*. New York: Pratt Graphics Center and Horizon Press, 1984.

Sledge, E.B. *With the Old Breed at Peleliu and Okinawa*. New York: Presidio Press, 2007.

Streicher, Lawrence H. "David Low and the Sociology of Caricature." *Comparative Studies in Society and History* 8, no. 1 (October 1965): 1–23.

Sunday Courier and Journal. "Green Pastures." November 18, 1934.

———. "Lions Offered to City as 'Real' Zoo Nucleus." March 18, 1928.

Sunday Courier and Press. "Daumier: A Pauper in Life, a Master in Death." February 14, 1965.

———. "Jannie Knecht." January 14, 1979.

———. "Karl Kae Knecht." July 30, 1972.

———. "Say Kay! Shows, N'Such by Karl Kae Knecht." February 7, 1954.

———. "Say Kay! What of Folks, Shows, Animals 'n' Such by Karl Kae Knecht." March 12, 1950.

———. "Start Fund to Buy Elephant for Zoo." March 17, 1929.

———. "Visiting Committee Plans Camp Program." February 20, 1944.

Thibodeau, Ruth. "From Racism to Tokenism: The Changing Face of Blacks in New Yorker Cartoons." *Public Opinion Quarterly* 53, no. 4 (Winter 1989): 482–94.

"Three Americans." *Life*, September 20, 1943.

"A Truly Amazing Production Record: 18,000 Editorial Cartoons!" *Indiana Business and Industry*, May 1958.

Tucker, Todd. *Notre Dame vs. the Klan: How the Fighting Irish Defeated the Ku Klux Klan*. Chicago: Loyola Press, 2004.

Turner, Martyn. "Confessions of a Political Cartoonist." *Crane Bag* 7, no. 2 (1983), 156–59.

United States Congress. *Congressional Record Proceedings and Debates of the… Congress*. Washington, D.C.: GPO, 1945.

United States Department of Labor. "U.S. Department of Labor—History—5: Progressive Era Investigations." https://www.dol.gov/oasam/programs/history/mono-regsafepart05.htm.

Vinson, John Chalmers. *Thomas Nast: Political Cartoonist*. Athens: University of Georgia Press, 2014.

Vogler, Richard A. *Graphic Works of George Cruikshank*. New York: Dover Publications, 1979.

Von Drehle, David. *Triangle: The Fire That Changed America*. New York: Atlantic Monthly Press, 2003.

Wachholz, Ted. *The Eastland Disaster*. Charleston, SC: Arcadia Publishing, 2005.

Wang, ShiPu. "Japan Against Japan: U.S. Propaganda and Yasuo Kuniyoshi's Identity Crisis." *American Art* 22, no. 1 (2008): 28–51.

Ward, Artemus, Christopher Brough and Robert Arnold. *Historical Dictionary of the U.S. Supreme Court*. Lanham, MD: Rowman & Littlefield, 2015.

Wartenberg, Thomas E. "Wordy Pictures: Theorizing the Relationship Between Image and Text in Comics." In *The Art of Comics: A Philosophical Approach*, edited by Aaron Meskin and Roy T. Cook, 87–104. Chichester: Wiley Blackwell, 2014.

Wathen, Patrick W. "Evansville Needs Grand Reminder of Its Efforts During War." *Evansville Courier*, August 27, 1995.

Weingartner, James J. "Trophies of War: U.S. Troops and the Mutilation of Japanese War Dead, 1941–1945." *Pacific Historical Review* 61, no. 1 (1992): 53–67.

Welky, David. *The Thousand-Year Flood: The Ohio-Mississippi Disaster of 1937*. Chicago: University of Chicago Press, 2011.

What America Thinks, Editorials and Cartoons. Chicago: What America Thinks, 1941.

Willard Library, Evansville Zoological Society and Mesker Park Zoo & Botanic Garden. *A Pictorial History of Mesker Park Zoo*. Evansville, IN: MT Publishing Company, 2011.

Wilson, Steven Harmon, ed. *The U.S. Justice System: An Encyclopedia*. Santa Barbara, CA: ABC-CLIO, 2012.

Woods, Marie H. "Knecht's Top Interest—His Wife." *Evansville Courier*, September 27, 1956.

Yoe, Craig. *The Great Anti-War Cartoons*. Seattle, WA: Fantagraphics, 2009.

Zeiler, Thomas W. *Annihilation: A Global Military History of World War II*. New York: Oxford University Press, 2011.

Zeman, Z.A.B. *Heckling Hitler: Caricatures of the Third Reich*. Hanover, NH: University Press of New England, 1987.

INDEX

H

I

K

L

M

N

O

P

R

S

ABOUT THE AUTHOR

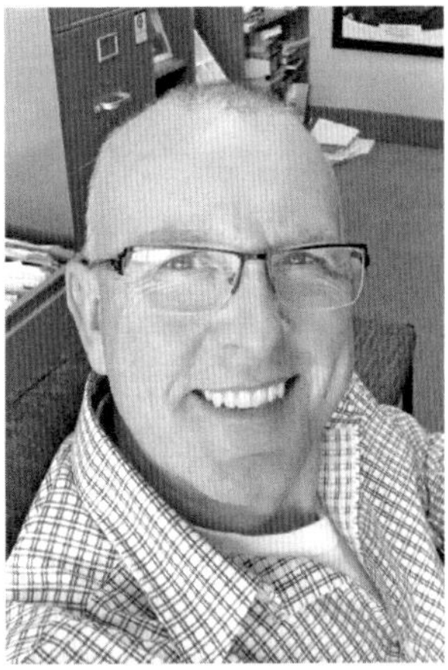

James Lachlan MacLeod was educated at the University of Edinburgh in Scotland. He taught history and British studies at Harlaxton College from 1994 to 1999 and since 1999 has been a member of the History Department at the University of Evansville. He conducts research and teaches courses in European history and the two world wars and lectures frequently on the history of editorial cartoons. He is the author of two books: *The Second Disruption* (2000) and *Evansville in World War II* (2015). He has written many other scholarly publications and in 2016 coproduced a two-part documentary for WNIN Public Television on Evansville in World War II. Dr. MacLeod has published thousands of editorial cartoons, most of them in the *Evansville Courier and Press*.